Humans

Text by
Pat Welch
and
Dennis Welch

Illustrated by
Mike Dowdall
and
Pat Welch

A FIRESIDE BOOK
Published by Simon & Schuster, Inc.
NEW YORK

Copyright © 1983, 1984 by Mike Dowdall and Pat Welch

All rights reserved
including the right of reproduction
in whole or in part in any form

First Fireside Edition, 1985

Published by Simon & Schuster, Inc.
Simon & Schuster Building
Rockefeller Center
1230 Avenue of the Americas
New York, New York 10020

FIRESIDE and colophon are registered trademarks of Simon & Schuster, Inc.

Designed by Main Street, San Francisco

Printed in Spain by Novograph, S.A., Madrid

10 9 8 7 6 5 4 3 2 1
10 9 8 7 6 5 4 3 2   Pbk.

Library of Congress Cataloging in Publication Data

Welch, Pat.
  Humans.

  1. American wit and humor. 2. Man—Anecdotes, facetiae, satire, etc.
I. Welch, Dennis. II. Title.
PN6162.W45 1984   818′.5407—dc19   84-13937
                              AACR 2   MARC

ISBN 0-671-53257-X

ISBN 0-671-60277-2 Pbk.

Humans

Introduction

The past several years have seen something of a flurry of published treatises on little-known phyla, families, or species which most of us had believed to be either mythical or extinct. In all cases the research has been thorough, the final works weighty and comprehensive. Comprehensive, that is, within the limits of the particular group being researched and reported on — and it is here that a serious gap exists.

However improbable any of the aforementioned creatures may seem, there is another, nearly forgotten race of beings whose *routine reality* is more astonishing by far than any legend.

For most of us, knowledge of the elusive creatures who are the subject of this study begins and ends with a few outlandish stories imperfectly remembered from childhood. Even among scholars, they have largely been relegated to the dusty archives of superstition and fantasy, dismissed as too unlikely to be anything but the whimsical creation of otherwise normal, rational beings.

It is neither our charge nor our intention to chide or chastise (in the language of our subjects: "badmouth," "dump on") our colleagues. Rather, it is to present our own findings, distilled from many years of research and observation, as objectively and accurately as possible. It is for you, the reader, to draw your own conclusions.

Consider, if you will, the human:

Where other beings scrape a meager living from nature, the human has largely replaced nature with cheap, comfortable, dirt-free substitutes. Humans *sell* nature to each other, for the hell of it.

Where other societies engage in various systems of barter for essential goods and services, the humans have so advanced this practice as to have completely eliminated the encumbrance of tangible products and services, and even payment. These have been replaced with convenient *symbols* of work, such as the "consultant," and with sophisticated abstractions of remuneration, including the "percentage of the net" and the "check (which is) in the mail."

Where other races are governed by kings or committees, the humans have done away with the very concept of leadership. Humans are fond of saying, "The *people* are the government" ("people" is the human word for "humans"). In the human idiom, this is the same as saying that the place is full of customers but no one's behind the counter.

These are only a few high points in the story of this remarkable and all-but-forgotten race. Though we have been conducting our research among the humans for some time now, it is far from complete. Much time and effort, for instance, has gone into the problem of simply learning to *think* like a human (which we have accomplished only imperfectly) in order to grasp some of their more advanced and elusive concepts. The fact is that we expect our research and our stay among the humans to continue indefinitely, and we do not regret any of the experience — with the possible exceptions of certain urban bus depots and the lobby of the Pink Pussykat all-night theater.

Nevertheless, we feel sure that when you have come to know the irrepressible humans as we do — and that, of course, is the purpose of this book — you will want to know more and more. This will probably necessitate, in addition to licensing deals for calendars, posters, T-shirts, coffee mugs, and, say, wastebaskets — another book.

And that, dear reader, is *your* first lesson in thinking like a human.

Meeting Ed

Brewski

Humans are, by and large, a shy and standoffish lot. While we have been tolerated during our stay among them, and even allowed to participate in certain rituals and customs, we have always known that we could never be really accepted as one of them. This fact would have put severe limits on our ability to interpret our observations, had it not been for one remarkable exception: the human known to us as "Ed."

Looking back, it is no longer clear whether we were first approached by Ed, or vice versa. In any case, we were soon on a very friendly basis, passing the first evening of our acquaintance buying each other many glasses of a favorite human beverage called (as we learned from Ed) "brewski." As we recall, we all ended up at Ed's apartment. (We may have been accompanied by some female humans, but somehow our memory of that whole occasion is on the hazy side.)

Since then we have visited Ed's apartment many times, whenever we encountered some particularly confusing human custom or artifact, or when we simply needed to put our notes and observations into some kind of perspective. We attempted to show our appreciation in the only way we knew, by bringing Ed as much brewski as we could carry up the three flights to his apartment. Ed was unfailingly generous with his time and knowledge, and always drank our offering enthusiastically, no doubt to spare our feelings by assuring us of the appropriateness of our poor gift. Often, our conversations continued into the small hours.

In short, Ed became our mentor as well as our friend, and his clarifications and explanations appear throughout the book, to the benefit and enlightenment of us all.

Ed, this brewski's for you.

After six or seven brewskis, Ed showed us his favorite tattoo, a traditional act of trust and acceptance among the humans.

General Characteristics

Humans come in a variety of basic colors, more or less as shown here. They make much of this fact among themselves, but we have been observing them closely for some time now and, frankly, they all look alike to us.

9

Human Genders

There are male and female humans. This much is known, but certain aspects of our research indicate that it may not be the whole story. Unfortunately, we have been unable to verify this, since we have adhered strictly to the scientific rule requiring a second sight-ing for verification; and it happens that every time one of us was conducting field research in, say, the Butch and Cheese Burger Bar, the other was across the street at The Iron Codpiece. Or vice versa.

The Spare Tire

Physically speaking, the most striking difference between humans and other better-known species is the "spare tire" (aka "roll," "love handle"). The spare tire is the ultimate mark of maturity in the male, and advertises to all females that they are in the company of a mature adult, easily satisfied and very likely over-insured.

Remarkably, however, our research indicates that this uniquely human feature may have another, even more important function. There is compelling evidence for the spare tire as the physical locus of much, if not all, of higher human thought. Consider the facts: virtually all respected human thinkers—network executives, wine columnists, self-help authors—sport the spare tire. But in every area of human endeavor (jazzercise, the Triathlon, Rocky's next title defense) where a tendency to think clearly, or even at all, is undesirable, the participants must first be *divested* of their tires/rolls/handles.

Some may put this down to coincidence. But they have not lived among the humans as long as we have.

Strength

The male city humans love to set themselves occasional tests of strength, yet get little real opportunity. So they have provided themselves with simple machines, found almost everywhere, which dispense little bags, as shown. These are made of a virtually indestructible material and promise, for the hardy few, a reward of food-like objects. When all the bags are gone, the city human will often test his strength on the machine itself.

11

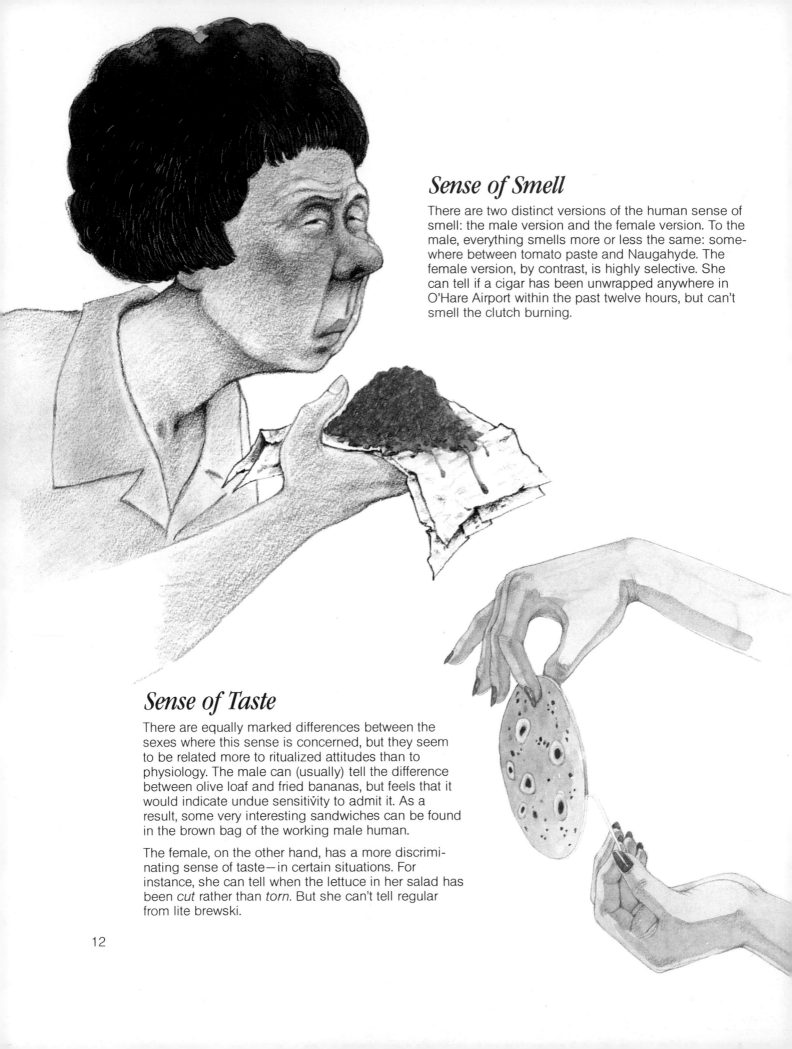

Sense of Smell

There are two distinct versions of the human sense of smell: the male version and the female version. To the male, everything smells more or less the same: somewhere between tomato paste and Naugahyde. The female version, by contrast, is highly selective. She can tell if a cigar has been unwrapped anywhere in O'Hare Airport within the past twelve hours, but can't smell the clutch burning.

Sense of Taste

There are equally marked differences between the sexes where this sense is concerned, but they seem to be related more to ritualized attitudes than to physiology. The male can (usually) tell the difference between olive loaf and fried bananas, but feels that it would indicate undue sensitivity to admit it. As a result, some very interesting sandwiches can be found in the brown bag of the working male human.

The female, on the other hand, has a more discriminating sense of taste—in certain situations. For instance, she can tell when the lettuce in her salad has been *cut* rather than *torn*. But she can't tell regular from lite brewski.

12

A male human who has dressed himself without female supervision →

Sense of Color

Again, almost exclusively the province of the female. It is she who decides the color of the drapes (sandstone), the carpet (champagne), and the appliances (avocado or harvest gold). The males are so devoid of color sense that they never interfere with—or even seem to notice—the female's selections. They know enough, however, to waste no time rubbing cigar ashes (charcoal gray) into the carpet (champagne).

Sense of Humor

Generally, anything pertaining to bodily functions, especially reproductive processes, or fooling other humans, especially one's spouse, humans find screamingly funny. To a human, the ultimate droll story would include all of these elements and take place at the gates of heaven, or possibly in a lifeboat. We've found the best course is just to laugh when they do.

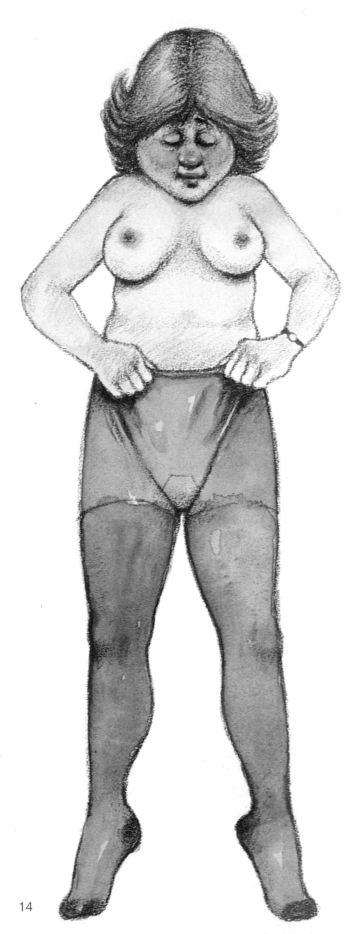

The Female

The basic female human is differentiated from the male primarily by a set of oddly distributed fatty deposits. And if there is one thing we have learned during our stay among the humans, it is this: you don't want to say that to a female human (*see* Language, p. 76).

Gravity is the enemy of fatty deposits, and therefore the enemy of the female, who has devised a variety of special garments to combat it. These become more specialized (and markedly more combative) as the female ages.

Among the humans themselves, these observations have given rise to the Theory of Gravitational Correlation, wherein it is posited that the force of gravity actually increases in direct proportion to the number of female humans who have decided to give up being in their late twenties. It is, however, only a theory.

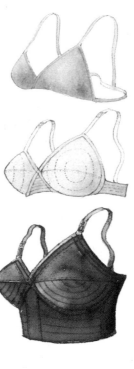

14

Sex Drive

This is an area in which the usually shy humans are not only willing to impart information, but virtually cannot be made to shut up. After months of copious note taking, however, it became clear that we were simply being kidded (*see* Sense of Humor, p.13).

What we mean to say is, if they've been doing all that they *say* they've been doing, then who has been paving the roads and putting out the newspapers? Gnomes?

Stages of Human Development

Infant

Principal event during this period is learning to walk. Baby's first steps are immediately followed by the learning of baby's first word: "No." The word is introduced by the parents in an effort to save the crystal ashtray, and the infant human quickly adopts it as his sole vocabulary:

"Baby want to go potty?"
"No."
"Baby want chocolate bunny?"
"No."
"Baby want to see another birthday?"

Diet for baby during this stage consists primarily of boiled tapioca, carpet lint, and small exoskeletal animals.

Child

Humans in this stage of development represent the entire human market for watermelon-flavored bubble gum, knobby-tired bicycles, chocolate cereal, and the artistic efforts of Sylvester Stallone. Fortunately for the purveyors of these items, this also sums up their entire range of interests.

Adolescent

The human in this stage of development is nobody's favorite person. His sister roundly despises him, though he believes that he chokes her far less than she deserves; his girlfriend's mother has compared him, unfavorably, with various reptiles; his parents unaccountably blame him for the fire in the station wagon. Adults tell him, "These are the best years of your life." He secretly believes this and is left permanently marked.

Young Adult

During adolescence, every human promises himself he will not repeat his parents' mistakes, by which he means their every thought and action. During the first three years of this stage, he duplicates every one of them exactly. Principal diet is glazed donuts.

Still a Young Adult

During this stage, according to all reports, nothing much happens; he doesn't think about anything in particular; he doesn't remember much about it later. It is usually adults in this stage who say to adolescents, "These are the best years of your life," thus demonstrating their general fogginess. Principal characteristic is glazed eyes.

Not Getting Any Younger Adult

Sometime after forty, male humans seem to emerge from their previous somnolence with a vague feeling of having missed something. Apparently, what they believe they have missed is Qiana shirts, pants without back pockets, and disco fever. Wives of humans in this stage develop a haunted look, as if seeing into the future.

Coot

This is the future. The human in this stage must be gentled out of leaving the house at 3:00 A.M. to "meet the boys"; keeps seven drawers of socks in the original store wrappers, and occasionally awakes with a start at dinner to shout, "Cleveland!" He will wear anything and always button it wrong.

Coot, obviously, is the stage to which all humans aspire. Venerated and admired by other humans, the coot is free from everyday drudgery as well as the shackles of social convention. The coot can have whiskey almost any time he wants it, for instance, and everyone merely smiles indulgently when he makes suggestions to his nieces for which other humans would be locked up.

It is clear that this relationship is mutually beneficial: those humans who keep venerated coots (or even codgers or geezers) in their homes demonstrate superior reflexes, unusually acute hearing, and generally increased mental alertness. You can see it in their eyes.

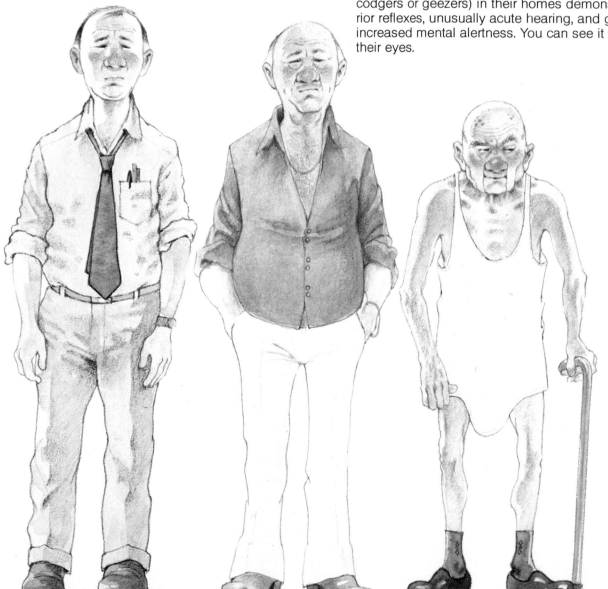

No human, of course, achieves coothood overnight. Below are the principal intermediate stages between middle age and the position of honor.

Facing page: Gramps decides to come to the party. →

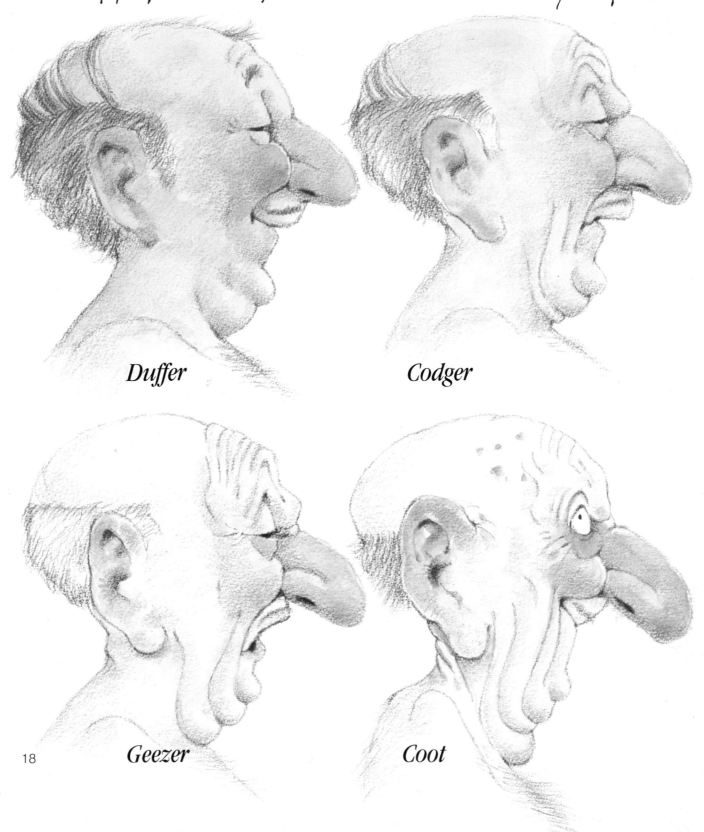

Duffer

Codger

Geezer

Coot

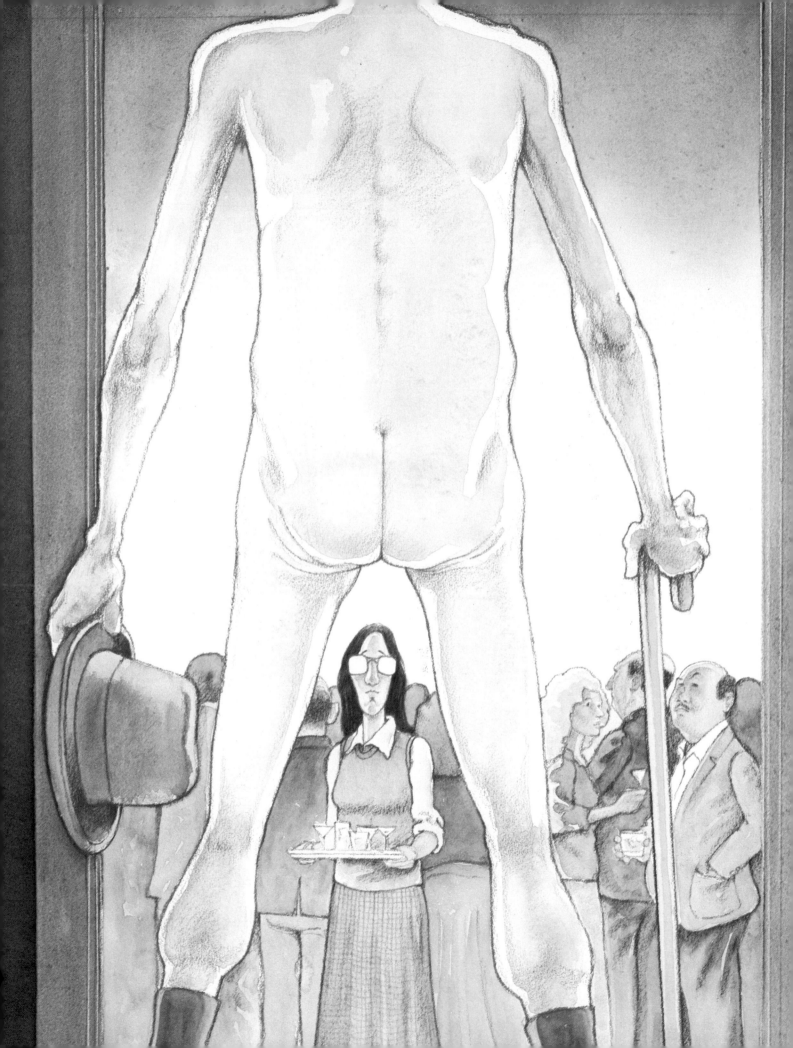

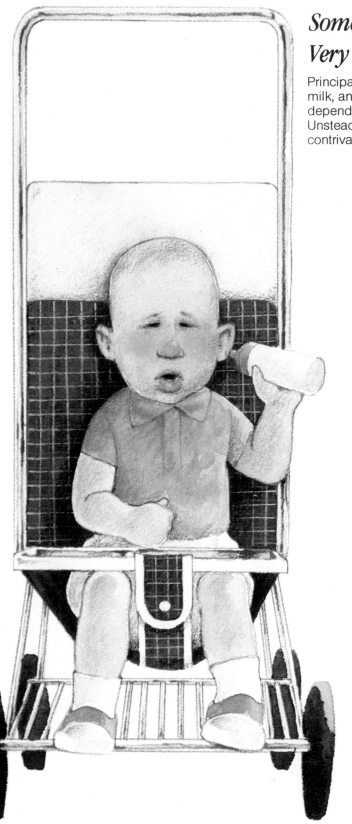

Some Points of Comparison: *Very Young Human*

Principal diet is strained spinach, bread softened in milk, and mashed bananas. Characteristics include dependency, incontinence, toothlessness, irritability. Unsteady efforts at walking are aided by mechanical contrivances. Often fails to recognize immediate family.

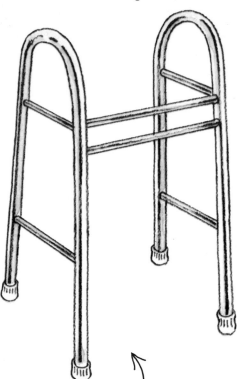

Above is the usual sort of contrivance used by the coot; at left, the type designed for the very young human. Occasionally, the wheels have been added to the coot's version, but this actually comes under the category of Human cruelty, to be dealt with in a later, longer book.

Coot

Principal diet is strained spinach, bread softened in milk, and mashed bananas. Characteristics include dependency, incontinence, toothlessness, irritability. Unsteady efforts at walking are aided by mechanical contrivances. Often fails to recognize immediate family.

The Adolescent

The intermediate stage of the human life cycle—adolescence—is designed to prepare the child for his or her entry into the world of responsibility, self-reliance, and steel-belted radials on credit which is the domain of the adult. This is accomplished by subjecting the adolescent human to six or seven years of utter rejection.

Physical Rejection

After a dozen years or so of unalloyed cuteness, the adolescent becomes, almost overnight, gawky and unprepossessing. The female begins to grow hair where she never imagined it, much less wanted it. The male fails to grow it where he not only expected it, but had big plans for it. The female becomes obsessed with the question of whether her feet will ever stop growing. The male's voice acquires a distinct honk, especially when he is agitated, which is more or less whenever he is awake. Both develop an inability to navigate furniture or doorways without injury.

Mental Rejection

Once they pass Introduction to Typing and master the operation of the trash compactor, adolescent humans conclude that there is nothing more to learn. On that basis, they develop opinions on global politics, nutrition, art, and the role of the feminist in Taoist writings. They do not develop any tendency to keep these opinions to themselves.

Chemical Rejection

The adolescent human's hormones are constantly in motion, but never actually arrive anywhere. Only three things ever happen to an adolescent:

1. Unjustly accused of something
2. Not listened to
3. Yelled at

Coincidentally, they experience only three emotional conditions:

1. Rage
2. Snit
3. Unbounded joy

The reader may, naturally enough, have a tendency to try to match items from the first column with those in the second. The parents of adolescents have the same tendency, for a while.

If this stage of development is difficult for the human experiencing it, it would probably be even more so for those living in close contact with it, were it not for the fact that fully seven-eighths of the entire term of adolescence is spent locked in the bathroom. This usually seems to be voluntary.

Parents of Adolescents

Interestingly, the parents of adolescent humans experience similar rejection syndromes. The difference is that while the adolescent human is more or less universally rejected, the parents experience it from only one source—their own children. Nevertheless, the patterns are remarkably parallel.

Total Rejection

At the onset of adolescence, the human child first notices his or her parents' clothing and hairstyles, and is appalled. By mid-adolescence, his attention has expanded to include the family car and furniture, the color scheme of the house, and the dishes. Toward the later adolescent years, the parents' conversation, politics, religion, and overall philosophical *Weltanschauung* has come under scrutiny and been found wanting. The adolescent keeps the parents apprised of the progress of these observations.

Types of Humans

Country Human

Seems to be slightly larger than city human, but this is because all country humans wear boots with high heels, probably to enable them to reach difficult pool shots. Impression of size is also reinforced by odd hat, which has no known function. It is easy to learn a country human's name, because it is on his belt.

Suburban Human

The suburban human lives a life of constant confusion. They live in a place which, while not quite city, is also not really country. This may explain why they are usually seen, while not quite undressed, not really dressed. During the day, everyone is gone except the dogs, who sleep. At night, everyone returns to sleep except the dogs, who bark. They (the humans) have extremely sophisticated electronic kitchens, and spend most of their free time cooking over an outdoor fire.

Mediterranean Human

This branch of the human family is extremely touchy and excitable, probably due to their invention of a type of coffee which is so unpalatable that they have also invented tiny little cups in order to avoid drinking much of it. They are inordinately proud of both of these inventions, and if you criticize either of them they will kill you. They consider it improper to appear in public with less than three days' growth of beard, so they shave every fourth day and spend the next three in seclusion. The experienced traveler can see all he wants of the Mediterranean during these 72 hours.

Teutonic Human

This group of humans has a reputation for technology, organization, and business acumen which is unrivaled in the human civilization. Unfortunately, they also have a penchant for odd little short pants and transvestite cabaret shows which prevents other humans from taking them seriously. Periodically, the frustration gets the best of them and they invade everyone.

Nordic Human

These unfortunate humans do the astonishing things shown because they believe it prolongs their lives. This may be true, but it is such a miserable way to live that their general distaste for these pastimes is reflected even in the roots of their language: a typical greeting is "Nörd ø fjörd," which means "Not the hell again."

Beach Human

This variety, indigenous to the west, has only rudimentary language and is never found in other human habitats for long. While other humans are often suspicious of the beach human, there is little to fear: the ineradicable odor of cocoa butter makes it impossible for them to sneak up on anyone. The name for these in the human language may be "sufburm" or "bumsurf." It is impossible to be sure because, in spite of the fact that they usually live in or near state universities, they have no written language beyond signing their names as part of a ritual called "endorse in presence of teller."

Teeming Humans

Marvels of adaptability, these humans are accustomed to crowds and have developed a number of compensatory traits. Their language, for instance, is designed to be shouted. Other efforts to minimize confusion include training themselves to dress and think exactly alike, and, since food shortages are a constant concern, to conserve supplies by attempting to eat with sticks.

Nomadic Humans

Most humans of this type inhabit vast, featureless deserts, so possibly the reason they never settle down is that they can never be sure whether or not they have tried every available campsite. They have a saying: "The camel is always browner beyond the dune." We have no idea what this means. We'd ask them, if we could.

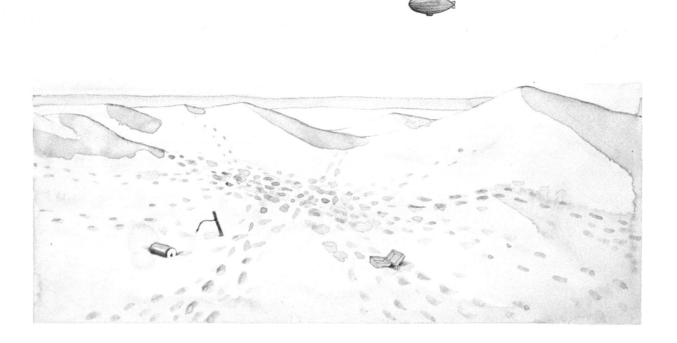

Elderly Female   City Human

Elderly humans like this one are much revered for their wisdom and experience. They readily stop and give advice — often at great length — to anyone they happen to encounter.

Male City Human

Appears to be squinting in sun, but expression is actually caused by recent introduction to future son-in-law

Odd hair placement probably to protect scalp from unaccustomed exposure to sun.

Approximate height when he leaves for work: 5'8½"

When he returns: 5'6"

Ritual tool case.

Feet turned slightly inward for efficiency in elevators and automatic teller lines, where the city human spends much of his time

Things written by and about other humans, which he believes to be true

Female City Human

Severely tailored suit counters femininity, conveys impression of aggressiveness.

Soft blouse counters aggressiveness, conveys impression of femininity

Shoes convey impression of having dressed in the dark

Height in heels: taller than her boss.

Out of heels: taller than the man she's dating.

white wine, whole chicken, wild rice, for show. Frozen burrito, for dinner.

Universally Unpopular Humans

The Civil "Servant"

This creature's natural habitat is a musty office with plastic chairs designed to fit only each other, and ancient Venetian blinds which have never been adjusted to admit sunlight. His clothing is usually drab and gray, like himself and his surroundings. His one pleasure is to stop other humans from doing anything, or at least from doing it easily. The chairs are for the other humans to sit in while they wait for him to tell them that they can't do it, that they must fill out Form 24-ZF9 explaining why they wanted to do such a thing in the first place, and then Form 25-ZF10 promising that they will think twice before trying it again.

The civil servant is not without cunning—it is nearly impossible, for instance, to comply with one rule without violating another—but fortunately he has no imagination and virtually never leaves his habitat.

Purveyors of the Light and the Truth and the Way

When any of these catches an unwary human at home, he is somehow hypnotized into standing and smiling and listening to interminable stories of the imminent end of the world. The Purveyors usually travel in pairs, ensuring that if one needs to take a breath between sentences, the other can immediately fill in, and the only way the human can stop them is to buy a little book containing the same stories he has just heard. The stories generally predict the end of the world within the week. The copyright date on the little book may be anywhere from three to eleven years old.

Most humans eventually escape and are none the worse for the experience, once their eyes unglaze. No one knows what happens to the humans who do *not* escape. It is said that they are made into Purveyors themselves, but this is probably just a tale to scare children.

THE METER MAID

It is this human's sworn mission to see that automobiles do what they are designed to do, which is move.

She considers this duty to be sacred, and when driving in a human city, even looking at a curb wistfully will often cause two or three of them to appear, as it were, at your elbow.

She sees it this way: if God had meant for humans to park, He would not have created loading zones.

THE WAITER

Human waiters are capable of expressing a great deal with no more than a look or gesture. What they usually express through these looks and gestures is that one's choice of wine, taken with one's request for A-1 Sauce for the veal, has reflected badly on one's genetic background and social desirability.

34

THE PETITIONERS

This group sets up card tables and placards in the vicinity of parades, donut shops, or any location where large numbers of humans may be expected to pass. They then assume that any human who _does_ pass must agree with their principles and prejudices, or would have the good sense to walk elsewhere, if not the decency to self-immolate.

THE MOVIEGOERS

These fun-loving types have seen the feature eight times, and delight in re-living the experience through shouted conversation. Their favorites are comedies because, since they have them committed to memory, they are able to laugh before, or even during, the actual payoff lines. During the slow parts they talk sports, if they have forgotten the radio.

Nocturnal Humans

If you go to a human carnival at night, he will be operating the Tilt·A·Whirl. During the day, he maintains a sexual relationship with the Tilt·A·Whirl.

This one usually gets the laundromat to himself.

The night clerk can hear a five-dollar bill hit the pavement a block away, but, strangely, never catches a name or notices gunfire.

This is an all-night convenience store. In here, at any hour of the day or night, humans can buy bread, milk, eggs, controlled substances, and automatic weapons.

Mellow Humans

Long-believed to be extinct, a few surviving groups have recently been discovered in remote coastal areas, wintering in cabins temporarily abandoned by non-mellow humans, and spending summers in L.L. Bean Superlite tents, paid for by the interest from their trust funds.

The males are characterized by full beards, shoulder-length hair, and colorful-yet-functional handcrafted clothing, which the females decorate with the distinctive designs of their tribe, usually flower motifs. The male's primary responsibility is the maintenance of extensive herb gardens, the locations of which are kept secret. They smoke pipes a lot.

When the females are not occupied with decorating clothes, making love to the sun, or meditating in celebration of freedom, they are usually nursing something.

Regional & Special-Purpose Clothing

Pacific City Human   Atlantic City Human   Village Human

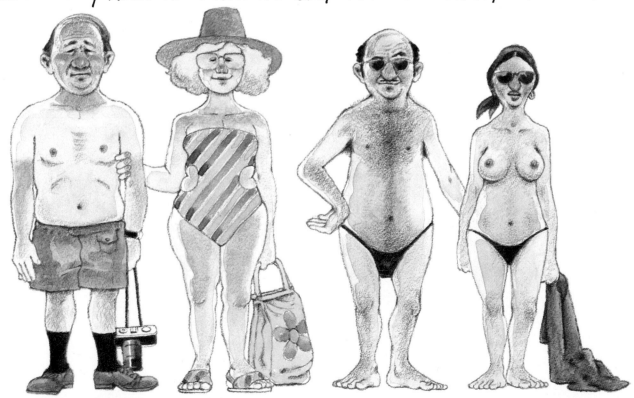

Recreational Dress of the North American Human   Recreational Dress of the Southern European Human

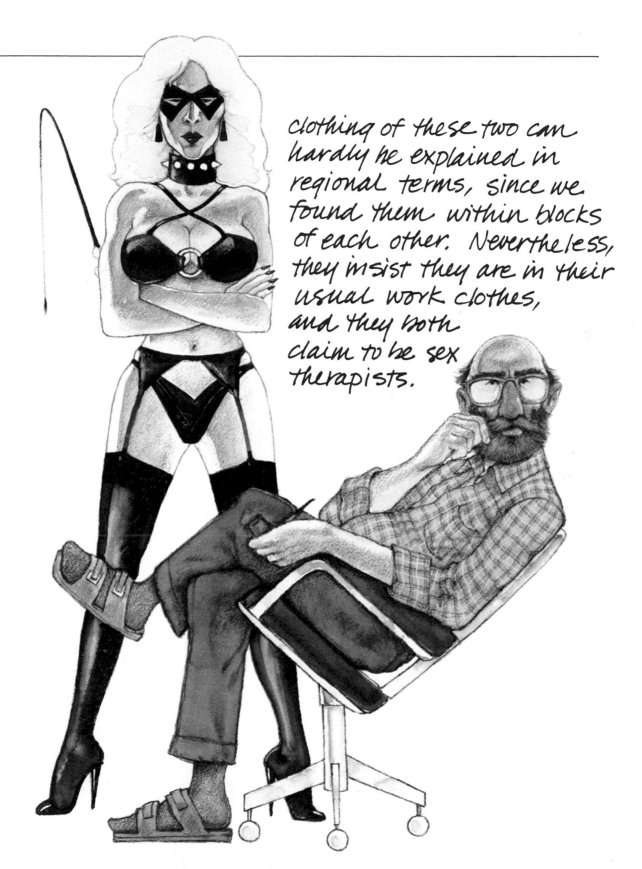

clothing of these two can hardly be explained in regional terms, since we found them within blocks of each other. Nevertheless, they insist they are in their usual work clothes, and they both claim to be sex therapists.

Example A.

We have no idea of the actual purpose of
but they must be very similar: whenever any human
gather, through which other humans circulate

Example B.

these two examples of special-purpose clothing,
appears dressed as either A or B above, large crowds
selling trinkets and souvenirs.

Human Leaders

Of all civilizations known to us, only the humans seem to apply really sensible criteria to their choice of political leaders: *beauty* (usually in both gown and swimsuit competition) and *talent*.

There are apparently many variations in the details of each district's political system. Some elect Queens or Princesses; others favor more dignified and understated titles: their leaders are addressed simply as "Miss Meat By-Products," or "Miss Honeydew Melons."

The details, however, are unimportant. What matters is that the humans' leaders are unanimously applauded and admired during their terms of office; none has ever waged a war of any significance; not one has ever been assassinated while in office; and the only recorded instance of graft or corruption concerns a candidate for the office of Miss Shopping Mall, who was disqualified when it was discovered that she was stealing toilet paper by smuggling it in her swimsuit.

There have been reports of obscure, isolated human groups who select leaders from among the *male* population, but this seems to us clearly preposterous. It is difficult to imagine any human voluntarily listening to endless speeches from a male aged somewhere between geezer and coot, without even the added interest of batons, much less honeydew melons. Common sense tells us that this is merely irresponsible rumor-mongering.

It is true that the speeches made by human leaders are not significantly more intelligent than those of the leaders of other societies. They are, however (and this may be more important), significantly shorter. Here are a few of the more memorable examples.

"If I were a tree—*was* a tree?—I would be, um, a really great *big* tree so everyone, regardless of racial affiliation, could have shade. Unless they live in a cold place and don't need it."

Nikki Honeyshank
Tuber City Potato Queen

"I will do my best in the coming year to be the best Queen the Okra Growers Association has ever had, to the best of my ability."

Sheri Periwinkle
Best Queen the O.G.A. Ever Had

"If I am chosen Picklers' Princess this year, it will probably mean more to me than anything else that could possibly happen to me this year. Maybe in my life."

Vikki van Cursive
Picklers' Princess

"I just wish everyone would love each other and not burn or otherwise destroy things, stores and things, and would just sit down and talk and stuff and maybe exchange small gifts."

Sandi Fairview
Miss Little Beach, Florida

"I consider it a privilege, not a right, to wear my tiara and travel everywhere waving to those who don't know who I am but came there anyway. Bless them."

Suzi "Silli" Chathwick
Miss Milk-Based Liquor Distributors

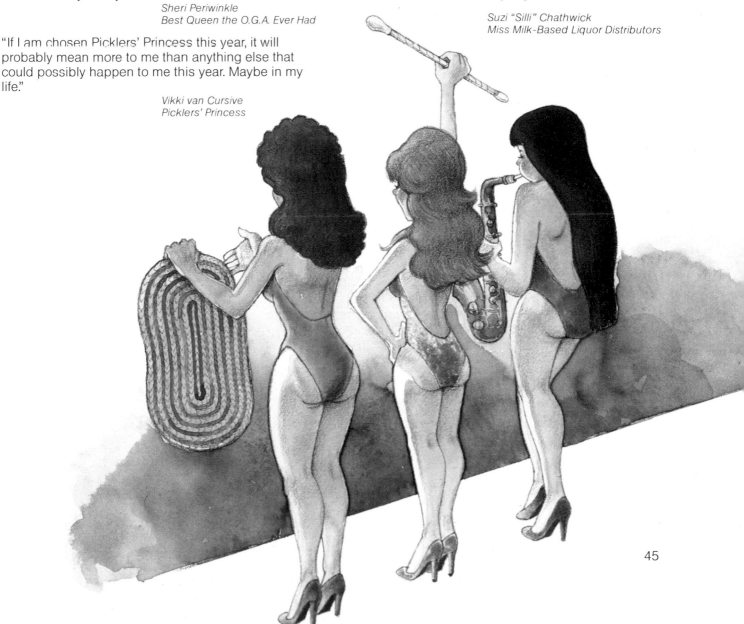

45

Courtship and Mating Rituals

For their first thirteen years, more or less, male and female humans take advantage of any opportunity to annoy or humiliate each other. That is about the extent of their interaction. They don't know why they do it, and they don't think about it much.

This changes with the onset of adolescence: the boys now take advantage of any opportunity to annoy or humiliate the other boys in order to attract the attention of the girls, whom they pretend not to notice. The girls, in turn, pretend to be surprised to meet the boys, even though there is no other likely reason for six fourteen-year-old girls to attend the National Transmission Expo wearing enough makeup to supply the Rockettes for three matinees.

So far, that is still about the extent of their interaction. The difference is this: now they *know* why they do it, and they think about nothing else.

Eventually, the more obvious of these pretenses are dropped and the males and females admit to a passing mutual interest. This marks the beginning of a remarkable and uniquely human ritual: dating. Dating is formalized training for marriage: it is designed to accustom the young human to be in the constant company of another human without spending an inordinate amount of time wondering why.

Since communication between humans must be a tricky undertaking at best (*see* Language, p. 76), and is literally painful for adolescents, one of the main objectives of dating is probably to avoid having to talk at all. The more nearly the young couple manages to approach this goal, the more they seem to enjoy each other's company. In this way, ritual dating advances into bona fide courtship.

Diagrammatical Example of Human Dating Ritual

Boy arrives at girl's house, is introduced to parents. He is asked apparently innocuous questions about, among other things, his career plans. He reveals that he is considering a degree in communications.

Elapsed time: 22 minutes
Words uttered: 17

Young humans go to movie, see *Revenge of I Drink Your Blood Part VII,* consume two Tubs o'Corn, two large Dr. Peppers, one $8 box of Milk Duds. Discussion of which was grossest scene.

Elapsed time: 2 hours, 31 minutes
Words uttered: 42

Young humans repair to Pizzas R We, secure table fourteen inches from 7000-watt speaker. Consume one large Special Combo with extra cheese, listen to latest release by the Stupid Dead Bunnies.

Elapsed time: 57 minutes
Words uttered: 12 (7 to waiter)

Young humans return to girl's house, remain in car for unknown reasons until girl goes inside.

Elapsed time: 36 minutes
Words uttered: 1

Total E.T.: 4 hours, 26 minutes
Total W.U.: 72

Ritual dating continues with only minor variations for several years until, at a prearranged time, the young humans are forced to participate in a sort of ultimate date which is called (as nearly as we can translate from the Human) "The Senior Prong."

The importance of The Prong to dating humans can scarely be overstated, and the preparations occupy much of their time and attention. First, a committee is appointed whose primary responsibility is to select a theme. This is usually something such as "Emerald Turnpike" or "Enchanted Standing Water." They then decorate a gymnasium or other equally unsuitable structure to reflect this theme.

Who will be the young human's date for The Prong is second in importance only to *what* will be the young human's car. Many delicate taboos apply in this area. Arriving at The Prong with the wrong date may produce stigmas which never completely leave the human in question. But arriving in the wrong *car* causes immediate and permanent loss of exactly that body hair which is most important to the young human. It has been demonstrated further that no human has ever grown any taller than he or she was at the moment of arrival in the wrong car.

The young humans, of course, must dress differently for the Prong than for normal dating, and it is in this area that they depend heavily on their parents' previous experience and present financial solvency. The parents, seeing their opportunity, provide the young humans with spectacular costumes which require teams of technicians to put on and (the parents fervently hope) to take off.

The young human couple thus sets out, resplendent in their traditional ceremonial costumes—which, by the way, have equally colorful names: the young male human's is called "the monkeysuit," and the young female refers to her shimmering gown (for which her parents have unflinchingly mortgaged the ChrisCraft) as "out of it for sure."

48

Arriving at The Prong in the wrong car

They first go to dinner, where everyone orders Surf'n'Turf. They then arrive at the decorated gymnasium, where they view the decor reflecting the evening's theme and ascertain that convention has been observed as concerns dates and cars. They may spend some time comparing gowns and monkeysuits and discussing the Surf'n'Turf. Occasionally there is some spontaneous dancing, but generally, once satisfied that the evening has not been marred by scandal, everyone is photographed and goes home. Exceptions include young humans who believe they have worked out the technical secrets of removing the ceremonial costumes. They drive to "the lake," if there is a lake nearby. In fact, they drive to "the lake" even if the only body of water within a hundred miles is the Petersons' new septic tank.

After the Prong is Over

Eventually, the young human couple's thoughts turn to matrimony. Whether this is at their parents' suggestion, or because they notice their friends doing it, or merely to save gas on trips to the lake is unclear. Whatever the actual reason, this is another situation in which the parents' financial solvency and sense of timing are crucial: announcements are generally printed and in the mail within hours of the young human couple's first shy statement of intention.

An unusually sophisticated example of Prong decor →

The Groom:

There is a human axiom which says, "Everyone looks good in a tuxedo." There is another which says that all axioms have exceptions. The bride thinks that he might at least have gotten a haircut. This is the direction her thoughts will take today.

The Best Man:

This is the groom's best friend or anyone who does not have a softball game that day.

Ushers:

Other friends of the groom or anybody who does not have a softball game that day. It is their responsibility to keep the families of the bride and groom separated and to drink as much brewski as possible without throwing up in the church parking lot. Or at least not in the church.

The Bride:

The groom has never seen her with her hair up, and therefore has never seen her ears before. At any rate, he has never really *looked* at her ears before. This is the direction *his* thoughts will take today.

The Maid of Honor:

This is now the bride's best friend.

Bridesmaids:

These were the bride's best friends until they found out who was to be Maid of Honor.

The Honeymoon

The honeymoon for the newlywed human couple is often provided by an uncle, and is usually in a place categorized either as "rustic" (the mountains) or "exotic" (the shore). The uncle would like to go someplace in either category, because he has spent thirty years in the garment district. The newlywed human couple has not spent thirty years anywhere, even if you count their combined junior college careers. They think "rustic" means a place without video games. They think "exotic" means a place with *new* video games. They usually opt for "exotic."

Dear Uncle Leo,
Here we are at
Maui Mel's. How
can we ever thank
you for this
wonderful trip.
Blair had 5
my-ties (sp?) at
Luau Night. The Sh
shrimp is fabulou
Your loving niece
Farah

OFFICIAL POSTCARD SOUVENIR OF MAUI MEL'S

54

Some forms of human housing are not what they seem—or at least, seem not to be what they are called. The human house at left, for instance, is openly referred to as a "mobile home," even though it never moves and its occupants go to great lengths to disguise the fact that it *ever could*. Another example: human guests in ordinary hotels are constantly coming and going; in the so-called "transient hotel," however, they seem to stay forever.

Some guests in the "transient hotel" hardly ever leave the lobby, much less the hotel. ↓

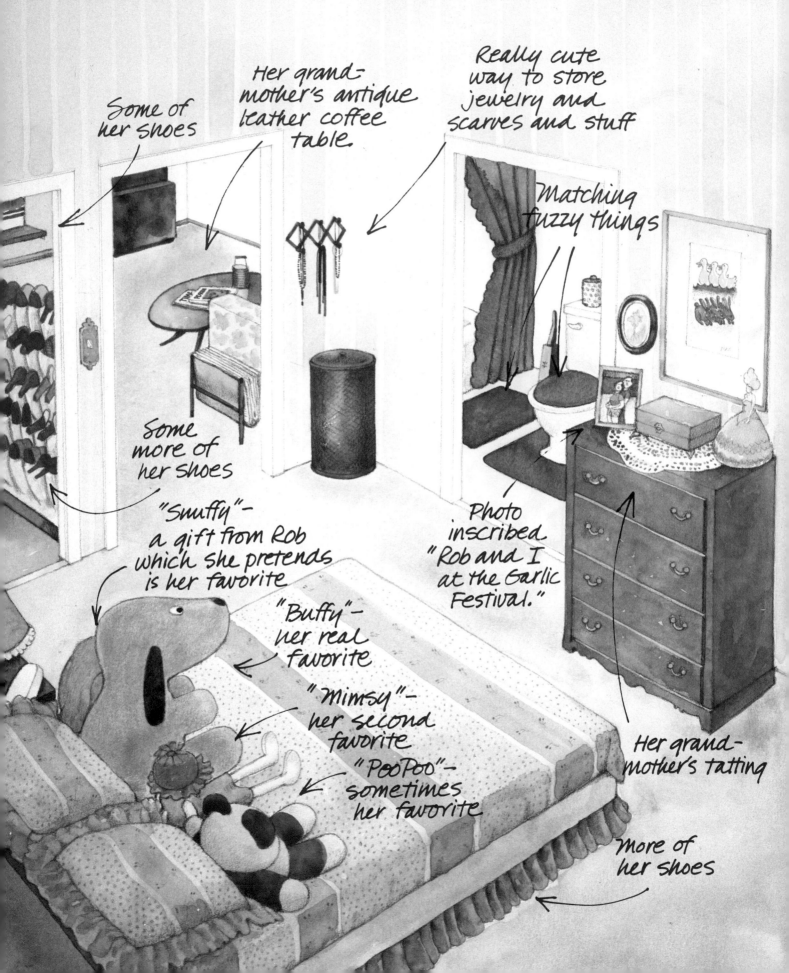

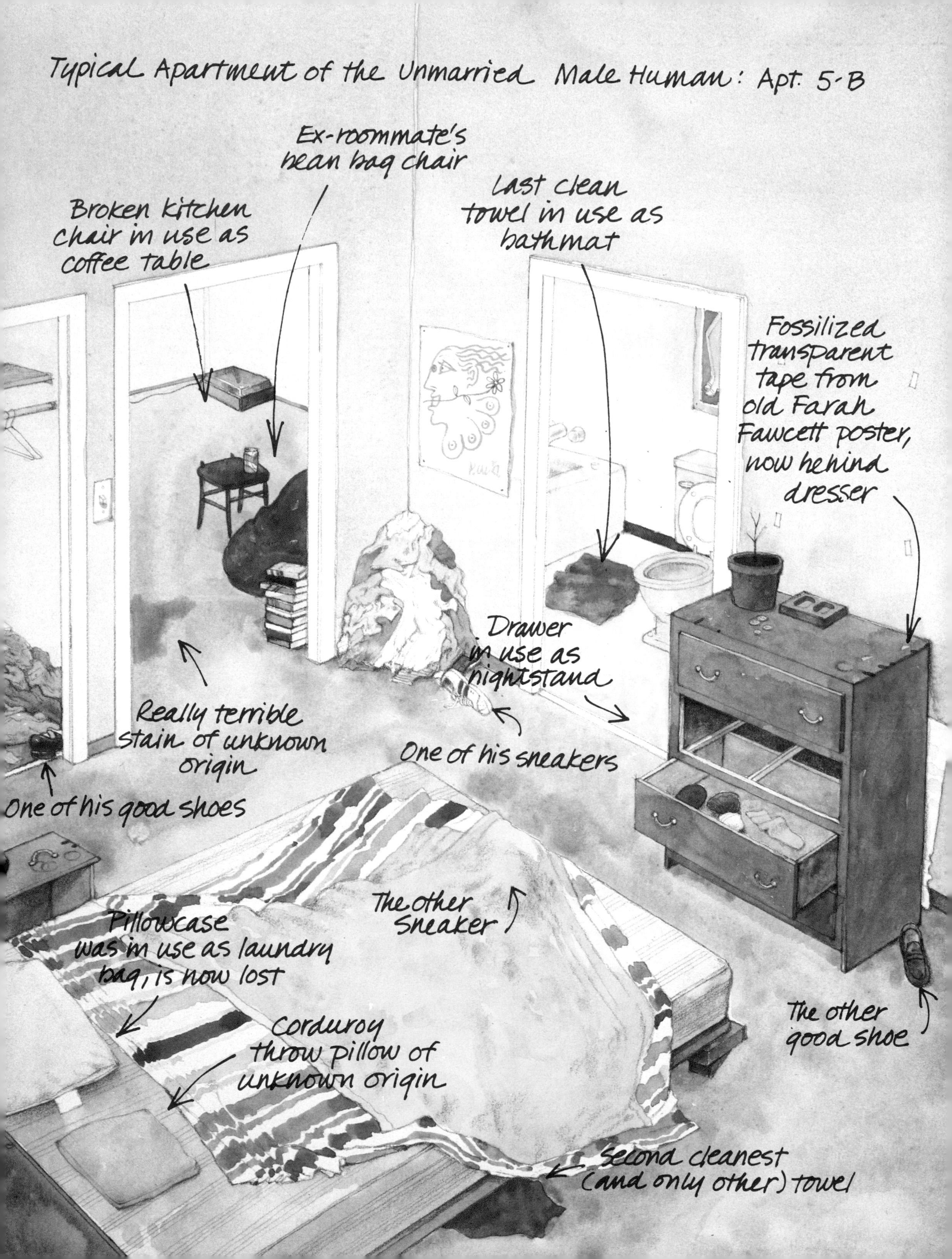

Typical Apartment of the Unmarried Male Human: Apt. 5-B

Ex-roommate's bean bag chair

Broken kitchen chair in use as coffee table

Last clean towel in use as bathmat

Fossilized transparent tape from old Farah Fawcett poster, now behind dresser

Drawer in use as nightstand

Really terrible stain of unknown origin

One of his sneakers

One of his good shoes

The other Sneaker

Pillowcase was in use as laundry bag, is now lost

Corduroy throw pillow of unknown origin

The other good shoe

Second cleanest (and only other) towel

The Realtor

This is one of the most important and respected of humans. Many humans aspire to Realtorhood, but the qualifications are stringent and the training rigorous: many human Realtors have completed six weeks or more of intensive instruction, for which they are required to buy their own books out of their meager earnings as computer repair technicians. Clearly, this is not a career for just anyone.

As is true of any society's shamans, the Realtor's payment is a matter of donation. His responsibility, however, is double-edged: he must find houses for humans who want them, and he must find *humans* for houses which other humans wish to dispose of, or, as the Realtor prefers to say, "unload." Toward this end, he asks one human what he wishes to pay, and asks the other what he wishes to *be* paid. He then communicates this information to the respective parties, who are so grateful for his service that one pays more than he had in mind, the other receives less than he wanted, and they donate the difference to the Realtor.

Though the training is demanding, no human is even nominated for Realtorhood without demonstrating certain mystical abilities. Minimum requirements include the abilities to magically banish dry rot and termites, and to determine, *without ever actually seeing them*, that the neighbors are deeply religious, go to bed immediately following the six o'clock news, and are unable to have children due to mismatched Rh factors.

A common type of human home is the "starter house," so called because of the definite jump, or "start," of surprise which occurs when the young buyers compare their first look at the place with the photograph taped to the Realtor's window. ⟶

58

What Humans Do

Anthropologically speaking, it is always fascinating to observe the ordinary daily routine of unfamiliar societies. Our extended time among the humans has enabled us to identify the daily activities that seem to be common to the greatest number of humans. It is reasonable to say, then, that what follows represents a fair picture of the average human's daily occupations and concerns.

Humans are ever alert for ways to improve their
situations or surroundings. At one time, one of the
most distasteful tasks of the city human was standing
in line in the bank, traditionally a stuffy and gloomy
place. The modern city human has done away with
this bother by installing mechanical tellers, which
(like the human teller) are perfectly efficient on those
occasions when they happen to be working, and
(unlike the human teller) emit endearing and
gratifying little noises when you operate them.
The main thing is, the mechanical teller
is on the *outside* of the bank. For the
human, this simple yet ingenious
advance means no more standing
in line in stuffy buildings.

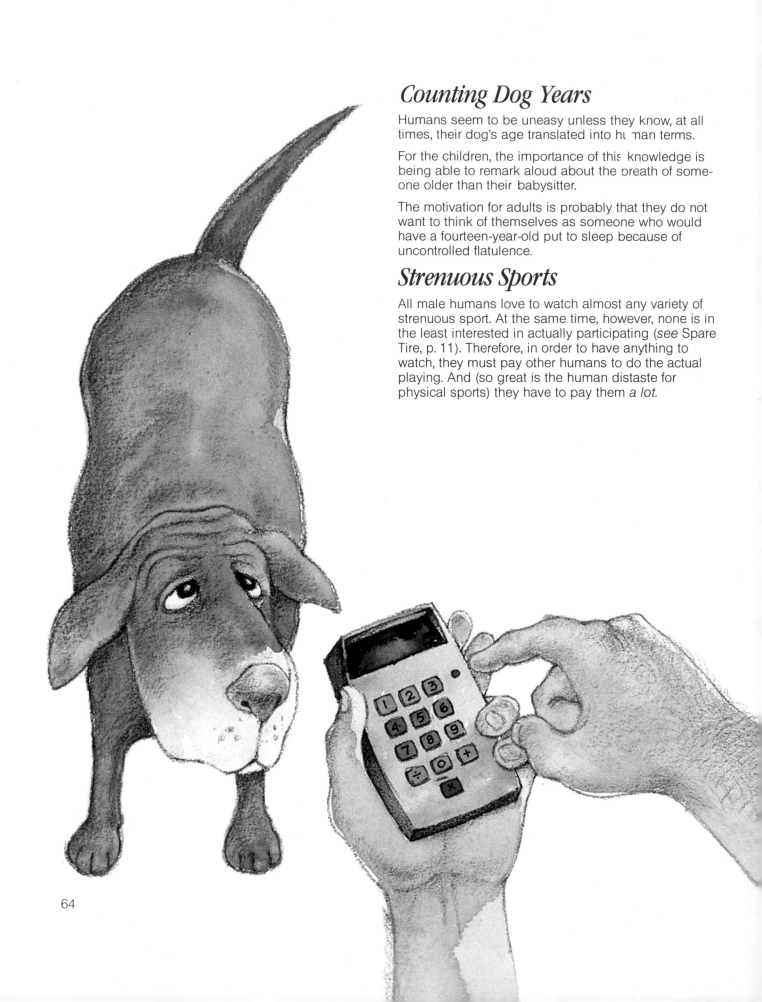

Counting Dog Years

Humans seem to be uneasy unless they know, at all times, their dog's age translated into human terms.

For the children, the importance of this knowledge is being able to remark aloud about the breath of someone older than their babysitter.

The motivation for adults is probably that they do not want to think of themselves as someone who would have a fourteen-year-old put to sleep because of uncontrolled flatulence.

Strenuous Sports

All male humans love to watch almost any variety of strenuous sport. At the same time, however, none is in the least interested in actually participating (*see* Spare Tire, p. 11). Therefore, in order to have anything to watch, they must pay other humans to do the actual playing. And (so great is the human distaste for physical sports) they have to pay them *a lot*.

The two humans above are among the unhappy group forced to participate in strenuous sports. As their demeanors suggest, large — even very, very large — amounts of money are insufficient compensation for their miserable lives.

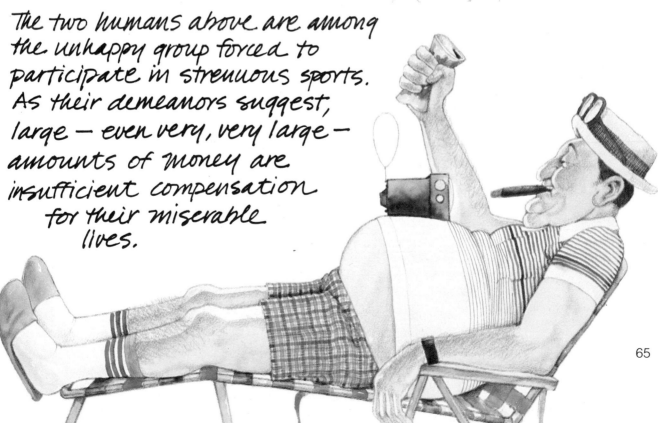

The Brown Paper Bag

The single most important object in the lives of the humans is, unquestionably, the brown paper bag. Not a day goes by in any human's life that he does not occupy himself in some way with a brown bag, whether to carry, cover, or scare the life out of something or someone (*see* Uses of the Brown Paper Bag, p. 68).

Every human household has a large collection of brown paper bags of every size and description which is constantly being added to. It is possible that the brown bag is the most important single measure of a human family's wealth. It is certain that one of the first lessons taught every human child is how to fold a brown paper bag correctly.

Correct Procedure for Folding the B.P.B.

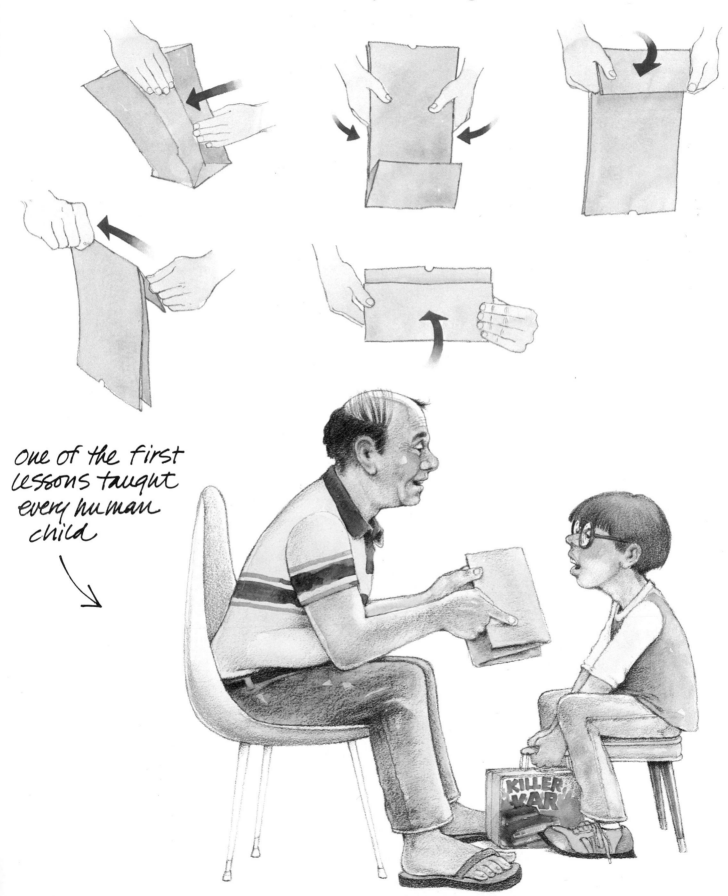

one of the first
lessons taught
every human
child

Humans use
brown paper bags for...

← Casual Luggage

Harmless Pet Amusement

Harmless Human
Amusement

68

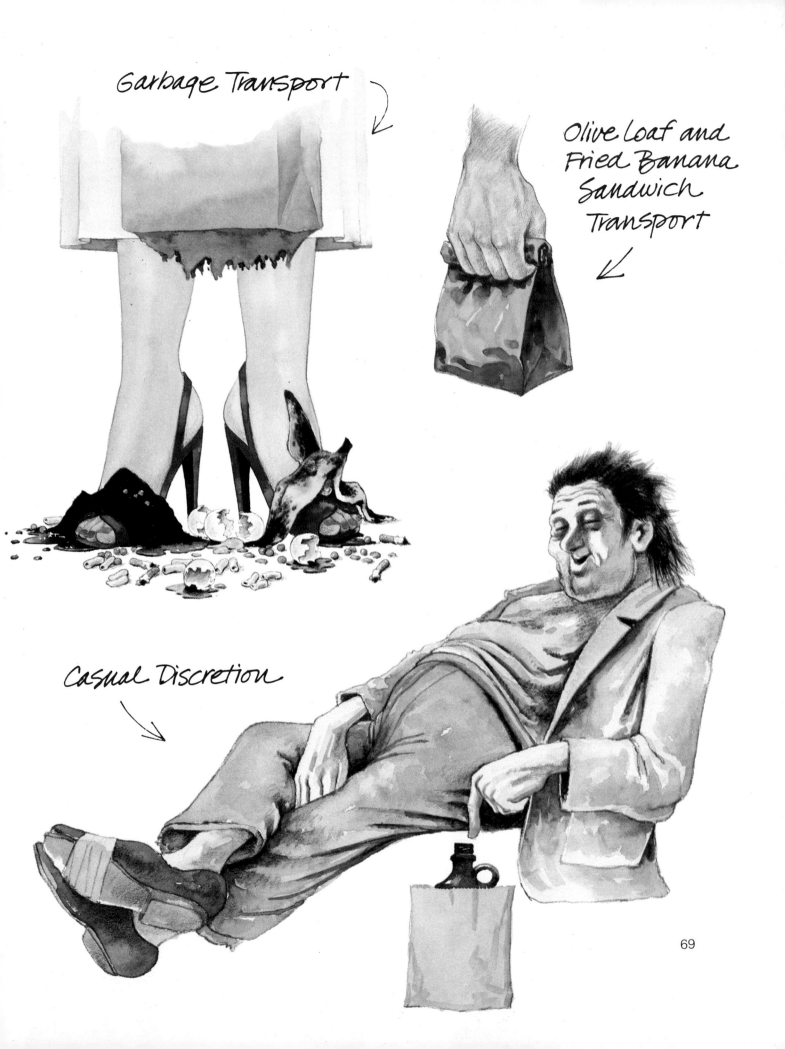

Garbage Transport

Olive Loaf and Fried Banana Sandwich Transport

Casual Discretion

69

Where Humans Go

The Laundromat

At almost any time of the night or day, you can find a human in here, though there are certain times when you might do as well not to look (*see* Nocturnal Humans, p. 36). It seems probable that the attraction which the laundromat holds for all humans is a throwback to an earlier age, when the washing of clothes was a major communal event. In those days, humans doing the wash did not speak to each other, either

NO TENNIS SHOES OR RUBBER IN DRYERS !

because attempting to get something clean with rocks is hard work or because they had not yet developed language. Modern humans do not speak to each other in the laundromat because they are aware that everyone has seen that all their underwear has no elastic.

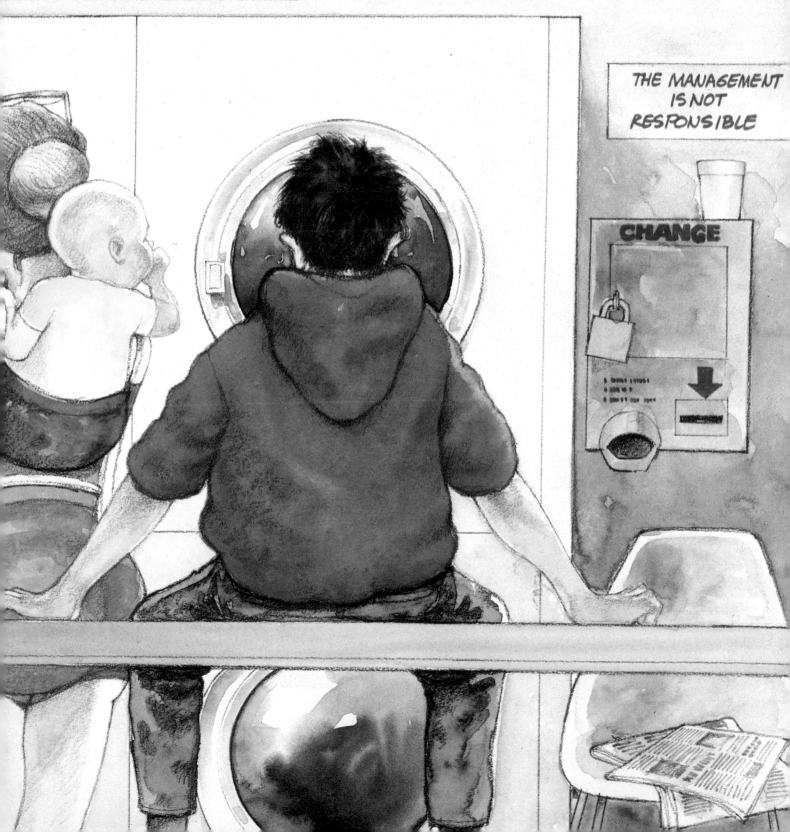

THE MANAGEMENT IS NOT RESPONSIBLE

CHANGE

The Office

This is by far the city humans' favorite environment. They cannot wait to get to this place every morning, and have been known to leave their breakfasts, ignore their children, and violate important municipal ordinances in their frenzy to arrive, or, as the human idiom has it, "pun-chin." While the attraction which the office holds for the human escapes *us,* its effect on *him* is obvious: once there, he visibly relaxes, puts his feet up, sips coffee, and reads the newspaper, until he goes to lunch. In the afternoon, he may change the locations of several pieces of paper (no doubt to vary his environment slightly for the next day) until it is time to return home. The real mystery to us is why, when the office is obviously such a congenial place to the city human, he is so punctual about leaving ("pun-chin-owt").

The Patio

These are places attached to human houses which are half indoors and half outdoors (*see* Suburban Human, p. 25). Though the cooking for the human family is traditionally done by the female, whenever they are on the patio (or "dek," as it is called by certain western subgroups) the male invariably does all the cooking, allowing the female only to clean up.

73

On every fifth corner of every human city or settlement is a donut shop.
On no corner is there a broccoli shop.

Human workers attempting to ingratiate themselves with their co-workers, bring boxes of donuts to the office.
No one ever brings a box of liver to the office.

While riding in the car, human children rarely, if ever, shriek, "Ohdadpleasepleasestopandget someboiledcabbageandnewpotatoes*please!*"

No doubt the pattern becomes clear:

Humans will eat anything.
Humans prefer donuts.

The Human Language

Learning the human language has been compared to attempting to describe a richly woven floor-length tapestry hanging in a dark room with an eighteen-foot ceiling armed only with a penlight without a ladder.

The reader may appreciate our dilemma: how to translate a tongue (which, inexplicably, seems to be the human word for both "language" and "sandwich") for which we had absolutely no point of reference. Certain helpful humans told us that what we needed

was a "Rosetta Stone," presumably a human linguist of some fame. Unfortunately, no one was able to help us locate her (if indeed she is still living), and it was finally necessary to abandon the search. Eventually, however, while cataloguing a group of obscure human artifacts, we happened on to the next best thing to Ms. Stone herself: a once-common object covered with words in human which, by easy inference, could have only one meaning each.

The closest we came in our search for the elusive Rosetta Stone was the lady at left, Ms. Rosella Stonebridge, assistant claims manager for Hugeco Insurance. Ms. Stonebridge was very nice about all our questions, but, as she put it, "I guess I'm no linguist, but I can tell you in this business I hear plenty of language."

Here is the object. Its actual function is, for our purposes, beside the point, and is in any case a complete mystery to us. The important thing is that each button bears a word in human and, since pushing each button causes the same exact thing to happen—but to happen *progressively faster,* it is clear beyond question what each word denotes.

Correct Human Phrases:

As is true of so many other aspects of the lives of the humans, their language, or sandwich, is rich with nuance and subtlety. It is extremely difficult to learn, and few *humans* ever really master it. In fact, the intricacies of enunciation are such that many human children are apparently encouraged to practice speaking while their mouths are stuffed with cinnamon toast or fried chicken. Or both.

Since even the simplest expression carries many possible shades of meaning, the result is dozens of words and phrases which all translate to exactly the same thing. This means, obviously, much extra effort for the student of Human, and it is effort which he shirks to his peril: to the human, what you say is far less important than how you say it.

Here, for instance, are a few phrases which all mean "Let's leave here and engage in sexual activity."

A. "Excuse me, is this place taken?"
B. "Do you come here often?"
C. "That's an unusual purse."
D. "I am studying to be a lawyer."
E. "I have driven here in my Porsche."
F. "I admire your fatty deposits."
G. "I am a lawyer."

Though they hardly include a single word of the root phrase, every human knows the meaning of every alternative phrase listed above to be "Let's leave here and engage in sexual activity." Furthermore, the use of any of the *alternative* phrases will gain you acceptance as a native human (though we cannot recommend phrase F); whereas, opening a conversation with the root phrase itself is likely, in our experience, to result in not being allowed to finish your drink. Much less your conversation.

For this example of the richness and diversity of conversational Human, we have chosen the simplest phrases found in any language, greetings and farewells, and listed a number of each, followed by the translations.

Greetings:

Hi.
Hello.
Hello, there.
How are you?
How have you been?
How do you do?
Hey how you?
How goes it?
How's the wife?
How's the wife and kids?
How's the family?
How's life treating you?
How's everything?
How's every little thing?
Nice to meet you.
Glad to meet you.
Pleasure to meet you.
Great to meet you.
So good to meet you.
I've looked forward to meeting you.
I've wanted to meet you for a long time.
Fancy meeting you here.
This is an unexpected pleasure.
Long time no see.
You're a sight for sore eyes.
It's been a long time.
It's been years.
It's been ages.
How long has it been?
Where have you been keeping yourself?
Where have you been hiding?
What have you been doing?
What have you been doing with yourself?
What's happening?
What's up?
What's new?
Que the hell pasa?
Say, mama.
Look, everybody, look who it is!
You haven't changed a bit.
Have we met?
I didn't catch the name.
We were just talking about you.
Speak of the devil.
Come here often?
May I see your driver's license?

Translation:

Greetings.

Farewells:

Bye.
Bye bye.
Goodbye.
Good day.
Good afternoon.
Good evening.
Good night.
See you.
See you soon.
See you later.
See you around.
I'll be seeing you.
So when do I see you again?
So long.
Later.
Catch you later.
Catch you around.
Bon voyage.
Have a good trip.
Have a good time.
Have a good day.
Have a good one.
Don't be a stranger.
Don't take any wooden nickels.
Don't do anything I wouldn't do.
Take it easy.
Take care.
Taking off?
Be good.
If you can't be good, be careful.
Sorry to see you go.
Leaving so soon?
Break it up here.
There's no one else, it's just not working.
Gotta split.
Gotta run.
Gotta fly.
Gotta go.
I'm late as it is.
Where did the time go?
Well, it's been fun.
Let me put you on hold for a second.
I'll get back to you on that.
Let's have lunch sometime.
Do you have a card I could have?
I'm afraid our fifty minutes is up.

Translation:

Farewell.

If the spoken human language has its pitfalls and surprises, nonverbal communication among the humans is even more treacherous.

Nevertheless, persistence at trial and error has made us familiar with some of the basics, as in these examples.

Right

Right

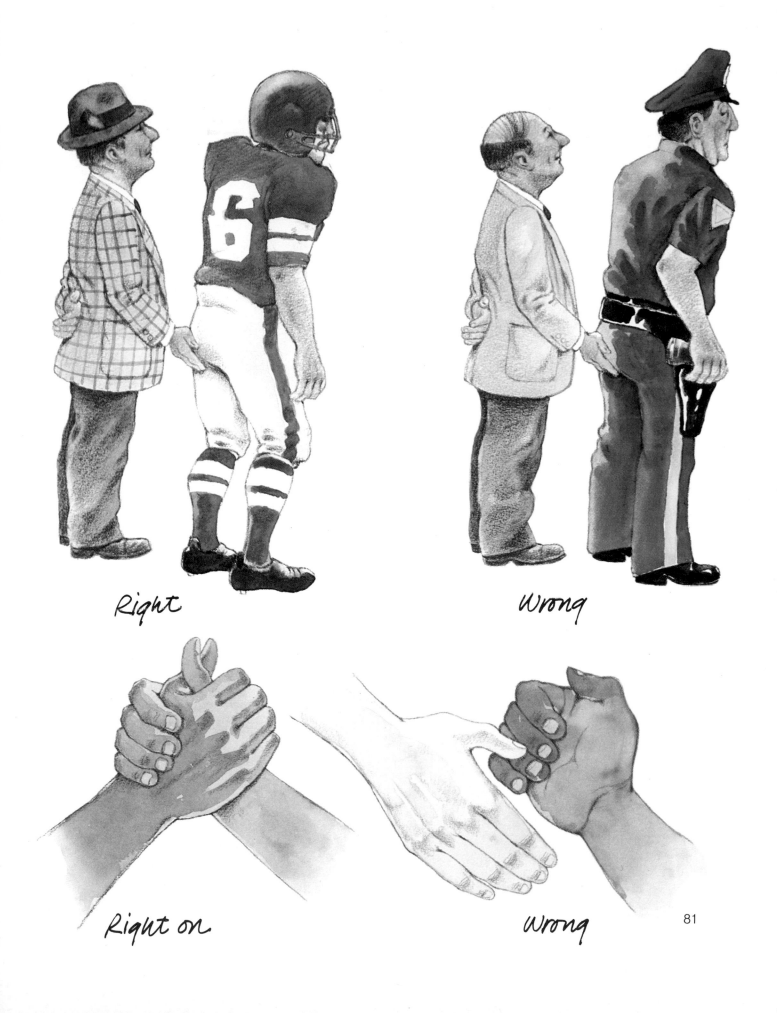

Right

Wrong

Right on

Wrong

Early Humans

The very first human forebears, limited by incredible timidity (and a brainpan that was nothing to write home about), spent virtually all their time gathering edible roots, grubs, berries, and whatnot. Anything else that they might have considered eating was either too fast or too big to be gathered, or had an unsettling tendency to view the human himself as edible. It follows that the diet of these early humans was exceedingly monotonous and bland. They had no word for Hollandaise.

More advanced groups attempted to enrich their culinary lives by the use of primitive traps. These had the effect (on small animals) of leaving little that was gatherable, much less edible, and (on large animals) of clearly pointing out the location of the edible early human.

Later humans improved greatly on both of these systems: they abandoned the traps and sent the females to gather the roots and grubs.

Even more advanced early humans (probably the true forerunners of the modern human) determined that there was no point in sending the females *out* for roots, grubs, and whatnot when they could all be raised right at home, which was where the females would obviously rather be anyway. This was a crucial turning point in early human history, for it left the males free, for the first time, to do what they liked best: hang around the fire, curse the weather, and tell each other lies about their early experiences with large animals. These were the first true human farmers.

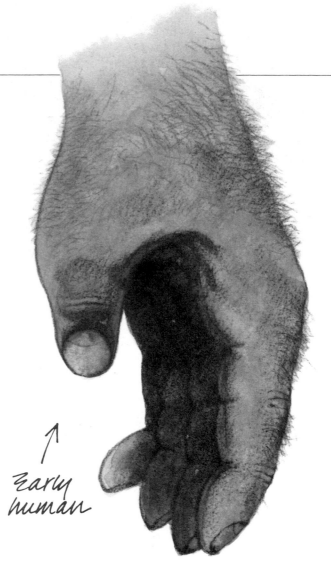

Early human

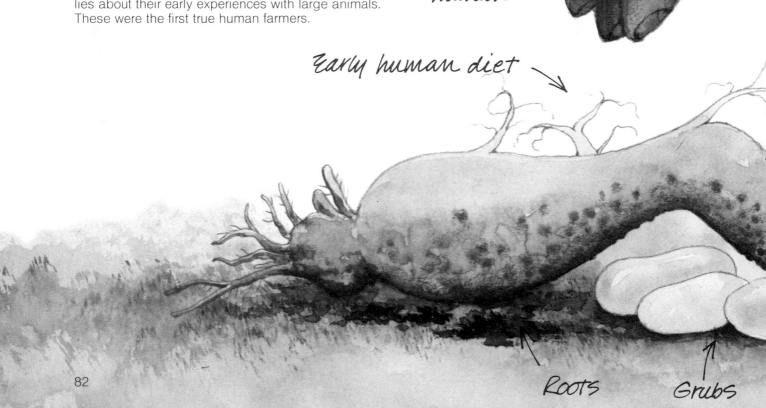

Early human diet

Roots

Grubs

Modern humans have, in every way, risen completely above their remote ancestors' dependency on the whims of nature: where once all was mud, modern humans enjoy cement. Where the primitives sought roots and grubs in their respective seasons, the modern human has Happi-Time Donuts, open twenty-four hours. Human farmers, who once could curse only the weather, may now curse the government. And to the modern human, nothing—animal or otherwise—is really inedible.

Early attempts at trapping met with no success — for the humans.

God knows

First human
ancestor stays
close to ground,
picks up food.
Gradually deter-
mines what is
food, what isn't.

Neo-synepherine
human observes that
best food is either
too big or too fast
to be picked up.
Complains, but
there is as yet
no government.

Neo-politan human
first notices other
humans, makes
effort to straighten
up. Invents money,
rudimentary trade.

First human has only rudimentary thumb, but is fascinated by it none-theless. Note flat brainpan.

Second epoch human has developed sloping face to provide easy view of ground, and pathetic expression intended to arouse sympathy in large animals. The first adaptation was fairly successful.

Next major evolutionary advance is in area of brain which controls pomposity. Note enlarged chest.

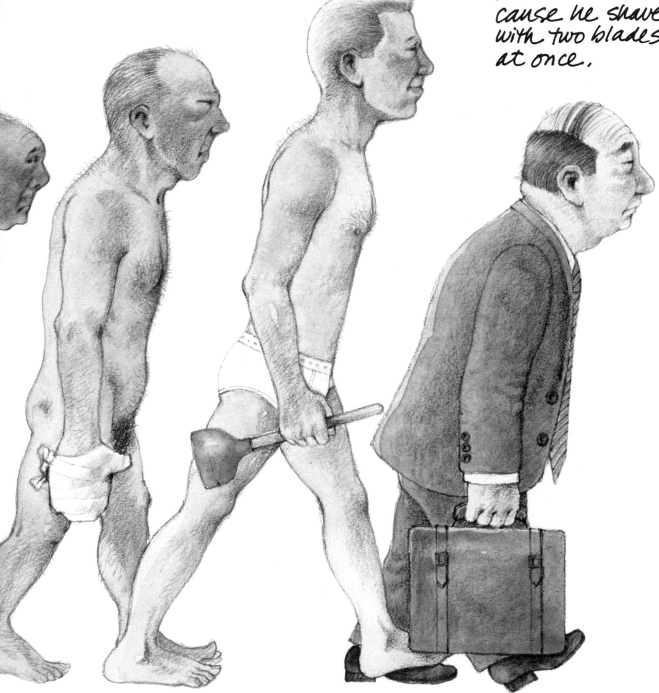

Cuppajava human invents fire, rudimentary bandages.

Pre-moderne human ponders nature, language, plumbing. Donuts are discovered.

Modern human enjoys ultimate brain development. Believes he is shaving twice as often because he shaves with two blades at once.

Increased intelligence motivates the Cuppajava human to question his lot. Considers moving to Portland, where he hears they're hiring.

Pre-moderne human is bored with thumb, becomes obsessed with his own brain. Affects haircut which accentuates brainpan—or, possibly, accentuates resemblance to Jack Webb (noted early human).

Modern human's brain convinces him that he is intellectual master of all he surveys. Begins to consider idea that he should stop eating dolphins and whales and (after a decent interval) begin conversing with them.

Evolution of the Female

No human has benefited more from the advance of civilization than the female human. The modern female human would scarcely be recognized as the creature who was once merely food gatherer, cook, maid, and childbearer, forcibly excluded from the vital and exciting arena of human events which was the domain of the male.

True, she still does usually do the food-gathering. And, probably, most of the preparing. And, yes, the serving and cleaning up. But these tasks are made immeasurably easier by the modern, enlightened male human's willingness to load the dishwasher. Obviously, she still does the childbearing. But where the primitive male human whiled away the hours of labor in some of his favorite pursuits—smoking, spitting, and reading male-human-oriented magazines such as Field & Breast—the modern male is made of stronger stuff. He puts on an

impossibly wrinkled green suit, complete with a silly, similarly wrinkled, little green hat, and stands beside the female until she delivers or he throws up and/or faints, in a touching display of willingness to share her discomfiture. But the most important difference is that, while the primitive female human was forced to fill her dreary days by visiting friends, watching over and playing with her children, or possibly picnicking or gardening, her modern counterpart is now completely accepted in the once-forbidden world of business. The modern female shares with the male the excitement of receiving quarterly performance reviews, memorizing sales tracks, fawning over abusive clients — in short, everything about having a career that is so gratifying to every human.

She's come a long way.

Primitive vs. Modern Shade

The primitive human's brow served the important function of providing him with constant shade. The modern human's greatly increased brain size has

robbed him of the protruding brow, but has allowed him to invent an ingenious replacement.

Primitive human's brow   Greatly advanced replacement

At some point in prehistory, the humans began to divide into two distinct groups: the MECHANISTIC, or physical, and the ARTISTIC, or sensitive. The former spent their time devising vaguely cylindrical artifacts in an attempt to make some use of their much-admired (by themselves) opposable thumbs.

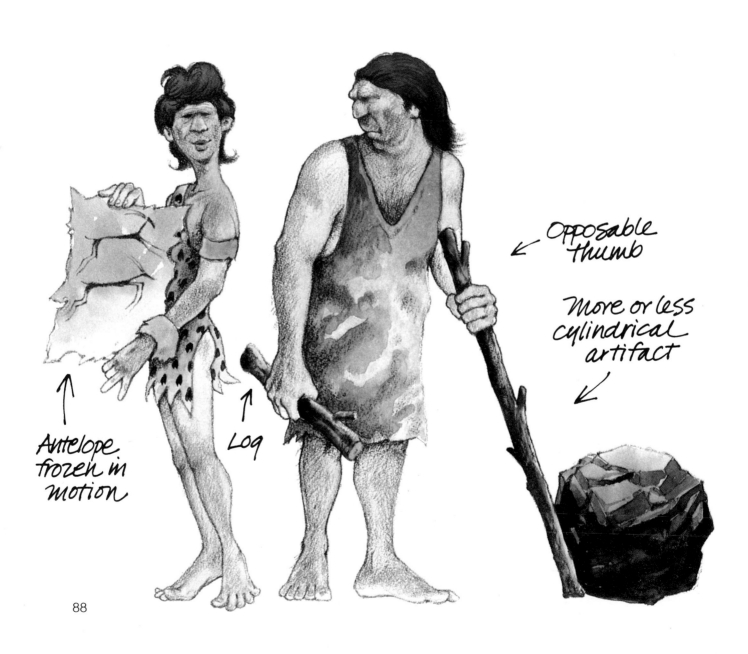

← Opposable thumb

More or less cylindrical artifact ↙

↑
Antelope frozen in motion

↑
Log

88

The second group illustrated the first group's large animal fantasies, covering the cave walls with improbably graceful bison, mastadons, and elk. For some reason, a deep mutual suspicion and animosity developed between the two groups which continues to this day.

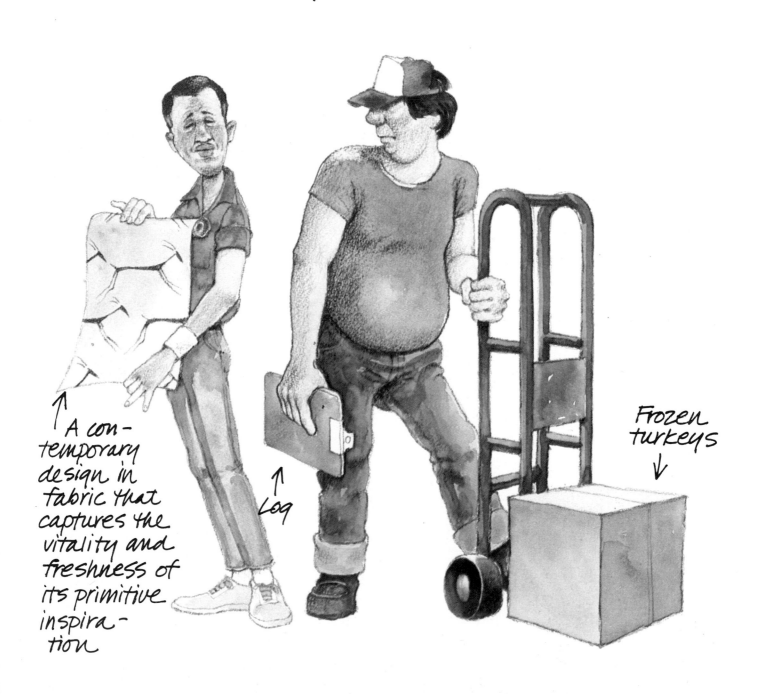

↑ A contemporary design in fabric that captures the vitality and freshness of its primitive inspiration

↑ Log

Frozen turkeys ↓

Mysterious structures such as this one have been discovered in several places where the primitive human population is thought to have been most dense.

Although their original purpose is unknown, it has been found that when the rays of the rising sun on the vernal equinox strike such structures, the shadow points directly west—long-believed to be a sacred direction among humans—indicating that they may have been intended as a sort of religious calendar.

Whatever the explanation, their haunting beauty is undeniable: an early work which continues to enrich the contemporary world of the humans.

Lost Human Arts

The Mechanical Shoes

Once universally recognized as the ultimate development in footwear, these shoes have become a rarity even among the oldest humans, and the secret of their construction is lost to antiquity. We are able to show a likeness and a diagram reconstructing their operation only after several protracted conversations with humans of advanced age who have kept faith with the old ways. Even they admit, however, that there were two places you didn't want to be caught with the mechanical shoe: 1. the rain; 2. the sixties.

Solidly constructed metal hinge is invisible when closed.

One of the humans who remembered the mechanical shoes →

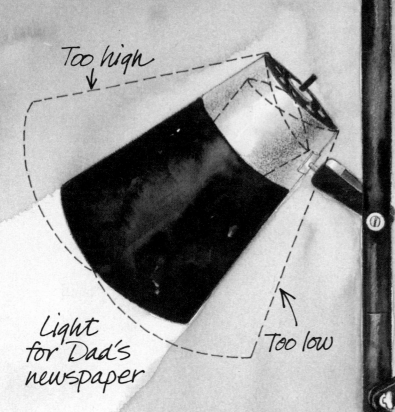

Too high

The Pole Lamp

Ingenious wing nut allows adjustment of lamp to any position.

Light for Dad's newspaper

Too low

Sturdy metal cones heat to 300° in under forty-five seconds.

Ingenious wing nut quickly becomes stripped — lamp hangs loosely

Light for children's homework

Light to bake dog or bleach carpet

93

This extremely functional form of
before the advent of the written language,

human architecture was developed
the sign having been added during a later epoch.

Humans and Nature

In primitive human times, trees and the like were everywhere, and every human came into more or less daily contact with them, as well as with moss, fungi, mud, humus, and so on. Clearly, the early humans were unlikely to have much appreciation for these (to them) commonplace items: no one is going to pack a lunch and drive twelve miles to visit humus when it is between his toes five days a week.

This state of affairs, unacceptable to the modern human, has been rectified with typical ingenuity: nature (and its various trappings) has been removed from the commonplace, and the best of it collected in remote locations. Humans—especially city humans—now are not only willing to drive great distances in order to view trees and humus, but willingly pay to park their cars in areas which were once covered with the stuff, thereby putting nature into the marketplace where many humans feel it should have been long ago.

No area of human civilization is more noteworthy than the special rapport which exists between the humans and practically all of nature's other creatures. While this mutual affection is always evident, it is probably most obvious during certain festive events at which humans dress up to resemble their favorite animals, and vice versa. It is truly touching to see chimpanzees, bears, and even parrots (though their taste runs somewhat to the garish) wearing human clothes, puffing big cigars, and pedaling little chrome-plated bicycles in open-hearted tribute to their human friends. Knowing the sensitivity and humility of the humans as we do, we were not fooled by their self-conscious laughter: we saw the tears.

Even humans who are compelled, for whatever reason, to spend their days in relative gloom will not force similar circumstances on their animal cousins, who are shown here enjoying a clean, well-lighted place. Note human at left, who has dressed like the fish even though this is, for him, no special occasion.

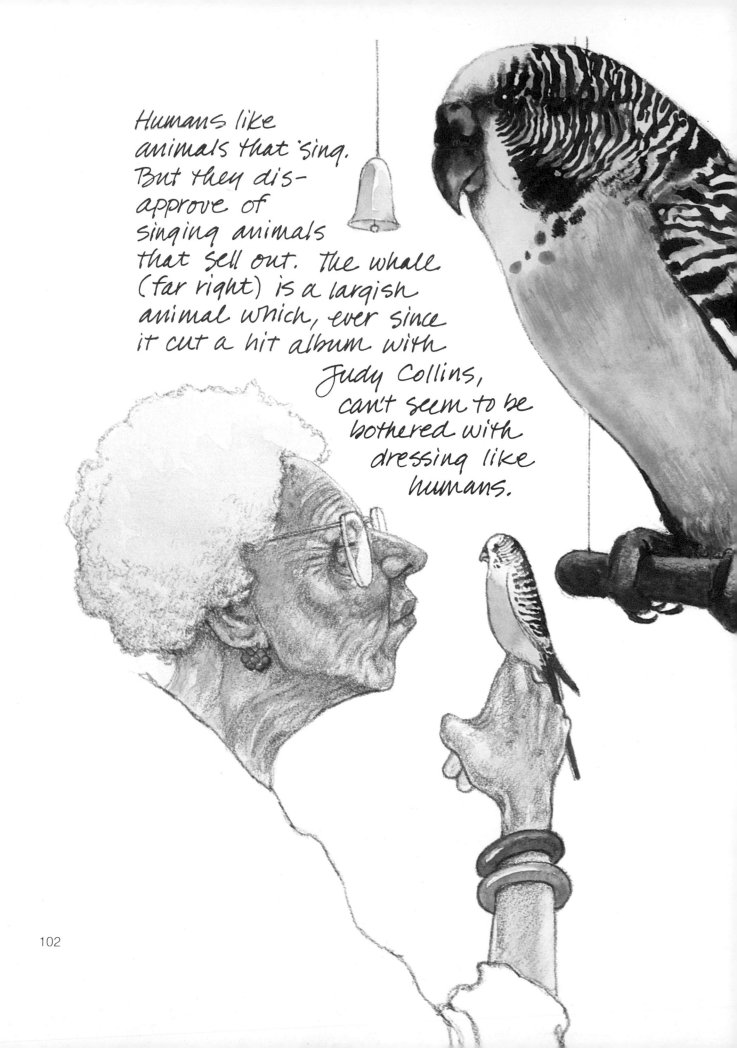

Humans like animals that sing. But they disapprove of singing animals that sell out. The whale (far right) is a largish animal which, ever since it cut a hit album with Judy Collins, can't seem to be bothered with dressing like humans.

On the other hand, the Budgerigar (left) sings its little heart out just for the innocent pleasure of singing. As a result, the Budgie (with a little help from the humans) sharpens its beak on the whale's bones. This may sound harsh at first, but an essential balance of nature is being maintained: you can't take a whale to Studio 54.

There are two notable exceptions in the story of mutual admiration between humans and animals. One is the dog, who insists on greeting humans in a way that the humans find, in a word, untoward, despite the fact that they (the dogs) have virtually all been taught to shake hands.

The second exception is the cat. Dignity is everything to a cat, and it is every cat's belief that any shred of dignity which can be taken away from a human becomes its (the cat's) permanent property. Cats rarely shake hands, and have been known to attempt suicide when forced to dress in human clothes.

Actually, there is a third exception: the Gila monster. The Gila monster does whatever it wants. (No one knows what the Gila monster wants to do, but everyone is willing to let it.) The humans don't talk about the Gila monster much. It will not shake hands.

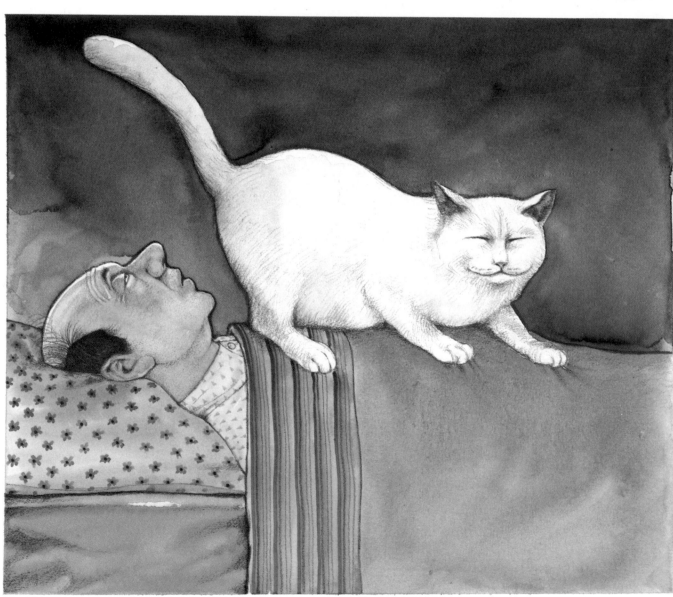

Secrets of the Female

The responsibility for the gathering, storage, identification, and preparation of food falls, as it always has, primarily on the female. She is uniquely suited to this task, with her far more highly-developed senses (*see* Sense of Taste, Sense of Smell, p. 12). But beyond these natural abilities, the female humans have also developed a large body of arcane knowledge, handed down from female to female and traditionally kept secret from the males, who are strictly excluded from the females' information-exchanging sessions.

A group of female humans exchanging information on the Magic Seal

Vertical meatloaf cozy

Of all their specialized knowledge, the greatest single advance in the art of food storage is what the females call the "Magic Seal." The discovery of this secret technique has so excited them that their information-exchanging sessions have very nearly turned into full-fledged parties.

Primitive version of the Magic Seal

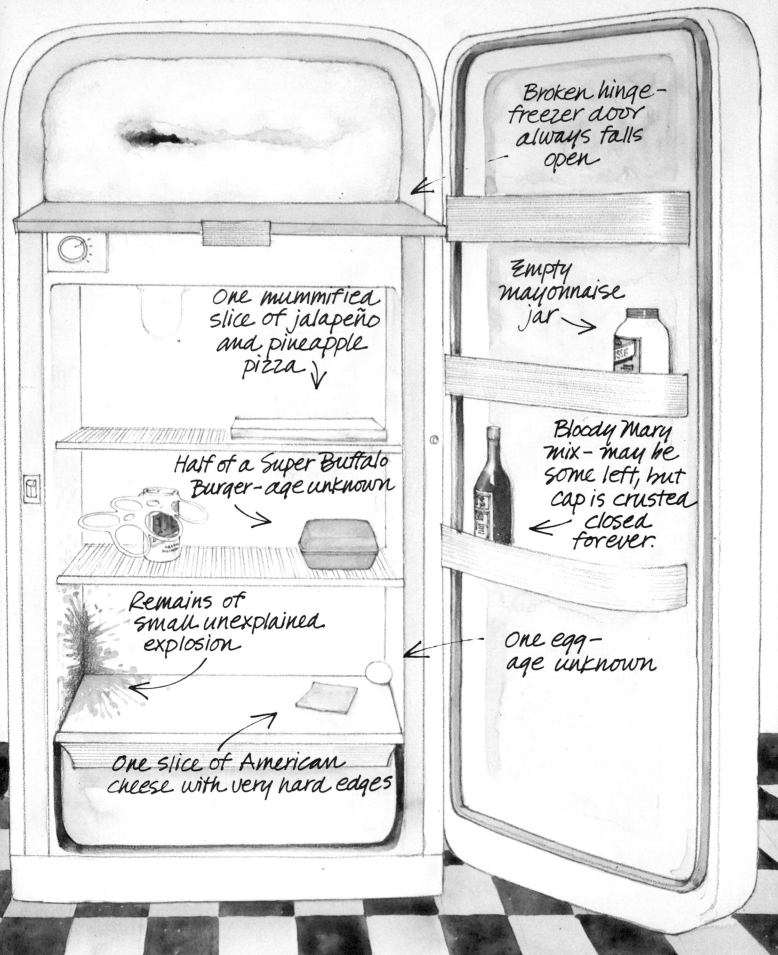

Low-calorie dinners arranged in alphabetical order

Chocolate chip cookie dough—half eaten (no cookies actually made)

Cheese log for little get-together she's planning

Baking soda

Low-calorie soft drinks arranged in chromatic order

Snowflake's favorite tuna buffet

The Magic Seal in action

Sense of Impending Doom

The female is only too aware of the male's tendency to drift off and not keep his mind on what he's doing. So a very good thing it is that she possesses this extra sense, which has prevented serious accidents more times than she can count, often enabling them to avoid dangers that no one else could see at all. As often as not, the male never knows what hasn't hit him.

Sense of Something Funny Going On

The female human possesses an unexplained—and unerring—ability to determine when things are not, from her point of view, what they should be: she knows when the male is not really calling from the office; she knows when the boys are considering doing something interesting to the cat; she knows what the children *really* do with their peas. This special female sense differs from the others in that it does not fully develop until she reaches motherhood, and it is apparently unaffected by distance.

110

Why the human female consistently out-bowls the male was a mystery until we discovered that they simply use a much lighter ball. The female knows that no human male will ever touch a pink or yellow ball,

and that therefore their secret—and their advantage—is safe forever.

The only mystery remaining is why they seem to have borrowed the males' shirts for this group pose.

Spontaneous Human Clustering

Spontaneous human grouping, or "clustering" as it is known to scholars, is one of the least understood of human characteristics. Whether triggered by a change in the climate, some ancient instinct, or a sound or vibration to which humans are uniquely sensitive is unknown. Whatever the cause, we know that individual humans periodically interrupt the normal patterns of their lives—sometimes donning odd costumes never seen at any other time—and cluster together, often in uncharacteristic attitudes, for periods ranging from an hour to a week. The participants themselves don't seem to know *why* they cluster; but they exhibit no more than normal confusion, content (so it seems) to wait for the grouping period to expire, when, as if by a prearranged signal, they all disperse and resume their usual solitary habits. Clustering is similar to (but rarer than) *milling*, a human behavior which we will examine in a later treatise.

114

An unexplained clustering of optometrists which occurred in Miami, Florida in 1974 ———>

Humans invariably demonstrate the spontaneous clustering behavior whenever another human, for whatever reason, attempts to leave the planet.

Human Rites

All races and societies possess some central belief or principle by which they guide the courses of their lives, and we had long believed that this must also be true of the humans.

Only our certainty that it must exist prevented our giving up the search before we finally found the central guiding ritual of the humans, hidden within the apparently casual activities of everyday life.

It is contained, typically enough, in a book. Every human home contains one of these books, and it is always kept in a special place. This is usually an ornate and imposing altar-like structure which occupies a central location—in fact, it is the focal point of the room. Though any member of the family is free to consult the book daily, it is the role of the male head of household to peruse it most extensively, and to quote certain passages aloud. This normally takes place in the early evening, with the family gathered in attendance. He will also occasionally make remarks which are not taken directly from the text, though they are certainly signaled by it. He might intone, for instance, "What *day* is this? What *day* is this?", at which the assembled family provides the ritual response, "Thursday! Thursday!" or whatever.

The book is, of course, written in Human. However, it is a form of the language which is encountered nowhere else, and includes liberal use of mystical symbols, numerical codes, and obscure cross-references. We are at a complete loss to translate, or indeed to make any sense of it at all. We have managed, however, to procure (at, we have no doubt, great personal danger to Ed) an actual copy which is reproduced here. Even without translation, it is a fascinating example of this most important human rite.

The book's special place is often the focal point of the room.

7:00 🞃34 **BASIN OF CULTURE—Documentary**

"Dixie to Cicero: The Jazz Migration" Part 28: Tubas and Snout Trimmin's: 1902–1905. The early Dixieland musicians find it impossible to meet women in the north who like the same parts of chicken as they do. Host: Rebecca Helper. Songs include: "She Be Big, Maybe Too Big Blues," "Can I Has Yo Fish?", and the classic "Wha's Dis on Yo Shoe?" Rare footage of Bigheaded One-Eyed Red performing solo on the Oxophone, the one instrument he never fully understood. (1 hr., 30 min.)

🞃17 **THE BIG OLDEST FAMILY—Sprawling Miniseries**

Part XIV: "The Waiting Madness." While Tom and Ira continue training their private army, Dr. Gladhand thwarts his sons' ambitions by falsifying the deed to the rain forest. At the same time, Crayfin, Swanto's son by his mulatto mistress, Crayfawn, buys a seat in Congress and begins a filibuster which could last well into Part XV. With Congress thus distracted, Crayfin's twin, Crawfay, corners the world market in corner mouldings and begins renovation of the family's country estate, Wyoming. Meanwhile, the recently widowed Mr. Guildkiller finally finds the courage to confront his headstrong daughter, Boradeen, forbidding her to marry the President-elect until she has done some picking up in her room. Dr. Gladhand: Sir Lawrence Snippet. Mr. Guildkiller: Ashen Pyle. Boradeen: Suzi Chathwick.

Additional cast:
Father Batrack	Landau Canteen
Tom and Ira	Biff Boyo
Mrs. Guildkiller	Lady Dame Broad

🞃4 **BAD DOGS—Comedy**

King and Prince eat the hamster's food by mistake and make frodo on the Jensens' new Lazy-Boy. King: Prince. Prince: King. (60 min.)

🞃TVA **CHAINED-UP CHICKS—Docudrama**

Stories of exceptionally beautiful women based on true cases of plain-to-ugly women in U.S. Prisons. (1 to 5 hrs.)

🞃ESP **GREEK RULES PIGGYBACK RACING**

7:30 🞃14 **DON'T CALL ME FATTY—Comedy**

Fatty crashes the Brewsters' dinner party and gets his head wedged in the freezer. Fatty: Tubs Velour. (60 min.)

🞃18 **FRISKY—Adventure**

An unidentified girl with a huge chest of diamonds appears at Frisky's door.

🞃TVA **IRISH RULES ROCKFIGHTING**

The children of O'Hannahannon Road versus the British "Flying Bee" troops versus the British "Flying Bee" troops cream of the Queen's Hearsay Waddlers Brigade. (2 hrs., 3 min.)

🞃11 **PAIR O'MEDICS—Urban Adventure**

Lungs and I.V. have reasons not to enter a particular downtown hotel.

🞃14 **REBUILT MAN—Good As New Adventure**

An embittered anti-vivisectionist steals Hodak's powerfoot.

🞃82 **IN DARKEST HOLLYWOOD—Documentary Filler**

A behind-the-scenes look at stars who stuttered or limped.

🞃32 **MOTEL DICKS—Drama**

Holiday and Ramada capture a young prankster who has removed the "L's" from the "Heated Pool" signs.

🞃61 **MIRACLE TELETHON—Religious**

The Real Reverend Billy Sol Muertes hosts the First Annual Miracle Telethon from the Miracle on the Mountain Broadcasting Castle in Miracle Mountain, New Mexico. Music and incessant prayer provided by the Holy Ghost Marching and Baton Chorale and the New Old Chapel Screamers, plus the inspirational comedy team of Mighty and Humble. Surprise testimony from Deacon Roy Don Rascal and the Big Cross Bears.

7:45 🞃9 **US AND NATURE—Documentary**

Topic: The Breaking Wind.

🞃10 **GIRL LAWYERS—Action Drama**

Trixie and Buns volunteer to walk through a rough neighborhood in their underwear in order to lure an arsonist/rapist from his hideout. Trixie: Rhonda Kibble. Buns: Leslee Cheek.

Supporting cast:
Arsonist	Miles Cheddar
Therapist	Ricardo McTavish
Florist	Armand Fello

⓫ DECOY SISTERS—Jiggly Action
Rosie and Tush must play volleyball in wet nightgowns to lure an arsonist/surfer from his beach hideout. Rose: Kitten Bean. Tush: Tress Tangler. Supporting cast:
Arsonist . . . . Big Red Torso
Detective Groaner . . . . Hale Fahr
Waikiki . . . . Santa Monica Beach
⓬ VERY OLD MOVIE AT 8
"Knuckles in the Navy." (1934) A mysterious three-legged dog befriends a one-eyed sailor on an old two-master. Dunce Barley, Lolita Tampico, Knuckles the three-legged mystery dog. (1 hr., 40 min.)
⓰ RANCHO MYSTERIOSO—Spanish Mystery
Miguel reluctantly enters the Federales' "Basement of Much Laughter."
❶ NEWS—Anson Trapweed
❾ AMIABLE ANIMALS—Nature
World traveler Ron Bearded gently nudges the sleeping pandas of South Bugetta in order that we may see their reactions, if any. (90 min.)
⓬ BEAT COPS—Action
Officers Kerouac and Ginsberg stake out a poetry session.
⓴ THAT'S GOTTA BE COUNTRY!— Variety
The Stiffleg Lanky Square Dancers keep up with medley after medley of country hits while host Toby Thresher drinks beer out of his hat.
㉒ THE INVISIBLE WEASEL—Special Children
Children tease a new girl in school until she makes friends with an invisible weasel. Story derived from Eleanor Rockne's "The Unseen Stoat."
❺ GRIMES, SPECIAL CONDUCTOR— Action
Grimes puts two and two together when several passengers are unable to produce transfers. Grimes: Somebody Familiar.
㏚ SALVADORIAN RULES CIVILIAN HUNTING
THE SHELLFISHERS OF SHEMP'S HEAD—English Comedy
The ghost of McGrodin's wife takes over his pockets at the pub.
MIGHTY CLERK—Mild Drama
Hamper battles an outdated file.

㉜ SCREW-UPS, PRATFALLS, AND SERIOUS ERRORS—Variety
Scheduled: screw-ups from "Don't Call Me Fatty"; real pratfalls from "Actual Folks."
BFD THE MIRACLE CONTINUES— Religious
The Real Reverend Billy Sol Muertes is joined on Miracle Mountain by the New Age Humming Pups, led by Bishop Patrick McFather, and the 1000-member Halftrack Glory Haulers performing the classic hymn, "Hey, You in the Valley, Can You See Us?"

8:00 **❷ BEST FORGOTTEN MOVIE— Comedy**
"I Can't Get It Right." (1956) Zany farce about a clown in Hell. Slappy Cackle, Fez Dante. (2 hrs., 10 min.)
❸ THE CANNIBALS—Comedy
Gramps secretly tries to fatten up the new family on the block. (30 min. on a side)
❹ I WEAR THE BRAINS—Comedy
Arlo hatches a scheme to make the dog lay golden eggs, but of course it doesn't work.
⓬ MALE MODEL—Adventure
An important assignment for a national underwear layout will be lost unless David can get a tan by 7:00 A.M.
❿ LIFE IN WEIRD PLACES—Nature
Rooter beetles and shovel dogs are hauled from their underground shelters and photographed under harsh lights. (60 min.)
⓲ WHAT'S WRONG WITH EVERY-BODY?—Comedy
Pop's newspaper turns up in the casserole one time too often. Pop: Henly Peckman.
㉛ MOVIE—Wise-Cracking Comedy
"Get Off My Lap." (1943) A fast-talking secretary uncovers a crusty old editor and just as quickly covers him up again. Reggie Astoria, Iris Hackett.

8:30 **⓲ THE VERY BEST OF THE ENGLISH STAGE—Pretentious Drama**
"The Codpiece" by Ben Whitepole (1636–1876). Live performance by the National British Socialist Puppet Theater, Strapped-in-on-the-Avon.
BFD THE MIRACLE ENDS—Religious
The Real Reverend Billy Sol Muertes winds up the Miracle on the Mountain with a medley of tributes to the Almighty by the Deafening Rumble Lipsingers.

Human Mythology

The Story of the Island

One of the most popular human legends concerns a group of strangers of disparate walks of life (a professor, a movie star, a millionaire and his wife, someone named Mary Ann, and the Skipper, too) who become marooned together on a small island. It is an epic in the truest sense: the original version took thirteen weeks to tell, and it has grown in the retelling to the point of being almost endless, as the story traces their efforts at survival, attempts at escape or rescue, and their antics as the diverse personalities interact. At first glance, it seems a simple—even vapid—story, suitable only for dull children. Closer examination, however, reveals that it is really a model of the entire human civilization, and great wisdom, both practical and spiritual, must be hidden beneath the surface nonsense. Almost all human children are familiar with this myth long before they begin school, and it seems probable that many base the actions of their entire lives on its moral and intellectual lessons.

The Little People

Among humans everywhere, the most common legend by far concerns some form of "little people". Invariably, they are rarely seen, generally benevolent (with exceptions), and better than, though very similar to, real humans. Usually they are said to live in the garden.

This is obviously an attempt to synthesize all the "best" human qualities in one humble and endearing—and mythical—group. A sort of reverse bogeyman, if you will, designed to provide wayward children and sub-sharp adults with a simple role model, while simultaneously giving vent to the teller's personal philosophy and private prejudices.

In all of our association with, and research into, the wholly remarkable lives of the humans, we have found only this one example of really insipid silliness.

123

Human Music

Human music is as varied (and as unintelligible) as human language. We have determined this much: different types of humans have specific musical preferences with which they seem to identify strongly, and which, presumably, reflect something of their characters and the circumstances of their lives.

We have matched our examples as nearly as possible to the types we have already covered (see Types of Humans, p. 24), and transcribed them phonetically. Feel free to sing along.

Country
(Whiney, but with a beat)

Ah usta have a job that got me through the day
Ah was workin' for the man;
 Ah was drawin' mah pay
  Had a good woman an' had a duplex too
Ah was jes like ever'body, Ah was jes lak yew
 Jes lak ever'body; jes lak yew.
  Well, mah woman run off with mah bes' friend
 Ah lost mah job, mah home an' mah land
But Ah'll bounce back; got a good job workin' night
Now mah job is Ah drink till Ah fight
What mah new job is, is Ah drink till Ah fight

Suburban
(High and breathy, with strings)

Giiiirrrrllll, I love the little hairs on your arm
Giiiirrrrllll, I love it when we can get real warm
Giiiirrrrllll, it's really nice when you shampoo
Giiiirrrrllll, I love you

Giiiirrrrllll, you're so funny when you laugh
Giiiirrrrllll, you're the ocean and I'm a rubber raft
Or maybe it's the other way around, but anyway
Giiiirrrrllll, I love you

Nordic
(Chanted, with horn accompaniment)

When once we burned thy shores
You pallid island bores
We cut off your hands and laughed
We cut off our hands and laughed
That's the kind of thing we did
Boy damn, it's cold here.

Mediterranean
(Loudly, with great emotion)

How can you have done this thing? You have irked me greatly.
One of us must die, it may be you.
Come, let us drink more wine and sing
More loudly so that all the village will know.
You have irked me greatly.
One of us must die, it may be you.

Teutonic
(Up-tempo, heavy on the tubas)

Tanks and trucks and tanks (ha ha)!
Tanks and planes and tanks (ha ha)!
Tanks and subs and tanks (ha ha)!
You took away our tanks (so what)?
We have some hidden on your flanks (ha ha)!
We would have won had our leaders
Not been crazy (ha ha)!

Mellow
(Sung nasally with electronically amplified accompaniment)

Hey baby, the city's too weird
The vibes are a hassle, there's food in my beard
Let's split to the country where everything's fine
You bring the stash 'cause I drank all the wine
But it's free like it should be, it's free all the time
You'll dig my old lady, 'cause she's got more wine.
Let's split to the country where everything's fine.

Teeming
(Chanted in an odd scale, with accompaniment by tractor and loudspeaker)

How we love to plant and plow under
The many words of our leader
We must be prepared to listen
We must be prepared to fight
We must be prepared for the future
We must be prepared to stifle the revisionists
Or be dragged through the streets
In large, floppy dunce caps.
We are talking big loss of face here.

125

Epilogue: A Last Conversation with

Our time among the humans, at least for now, was drawing to a close. We had seen and experienced—and certainly learned—a great deal, and felt that we could confidently say that we had come to know and understand the lives of the humans as few have ever done.

But there was also much that was unexplained and, as we had done so many times before when answers or understanding eluded us, we turned to Ed.

Though we knew we may well have been climbing Ed's steps for the last time, a case of brewski under each arm, there was an air of anticipation which offset the sadness: a sense that tonight there may be things we would hear for the *first* time.

Once the usual amenities were dispensed with, and we had a brewski or two, as it is said in Human, "below the belt," we came to the point.

"Ed, you know we have to be leaving soon."

"Sure, boys, I know how it is. Gotta move on. Well, you're young yet, I know how it is."

"And we want you to know how much we appreciate all your help."

"Hey, hey, nothin' to it. Day nodda, as they say." (We have no idea who says "day nodda," or what it means, but we thought it best not to press Ed on this point.—Ed.)

"But we have a few questions."

"Questions, well hey. Ask away, as they say."

"Well—"

"Say, I've got a question. Who's ready for another brewski?"

"Not yet, Ed, thanks. We're fine."

"Okay. Talk ahead, boys."

"Well, one question is how did the female develop so many more senses than the male?"

"Well, now. That's a pretty good one. I don't know *how* they got 'em, but it's dollars to donuts they got 'em all right. Y' know, you're not supposed to be able to smell vodka on anybody's breath, but damned if my first wife—"

"What about the language, Ed?"

"Oh. 'Scuse my French."

"No, no, the *human* language. For instance, why so many ways to say the same thing?"

"Well, you know, it's not what you say, it's the way that you say it, as they say."

"Yes, but why?"

"Why what? Listen, I got some chop suey left here—"

"No, no thanks, Ed."

"Sure?"

"Sure."

"Okay. Where were we?"

"Well, Ed, we'd like to know—"

"Hey. You wanta know about this tattoo?"

"No. I mean, yes, but we already—what we mean is we *do* want to know about it, Ed, but not right now, if you don't mind."

"Hey, hey. Forget it. Whatever you wanta know, well hey, you just shoot."

"Thanks, Ed, for understanding. Now, these are things that our readers are going to want to know—that they will *demand* to know, Ed, and our time is short."

"How's your brewski?"

"Good, Ed, it's fine."

"More chips?"

"Uh—plenty of chips here, Ed, but—"

"You sure about that chop suey?"

"Ed, please. Our time is running out."

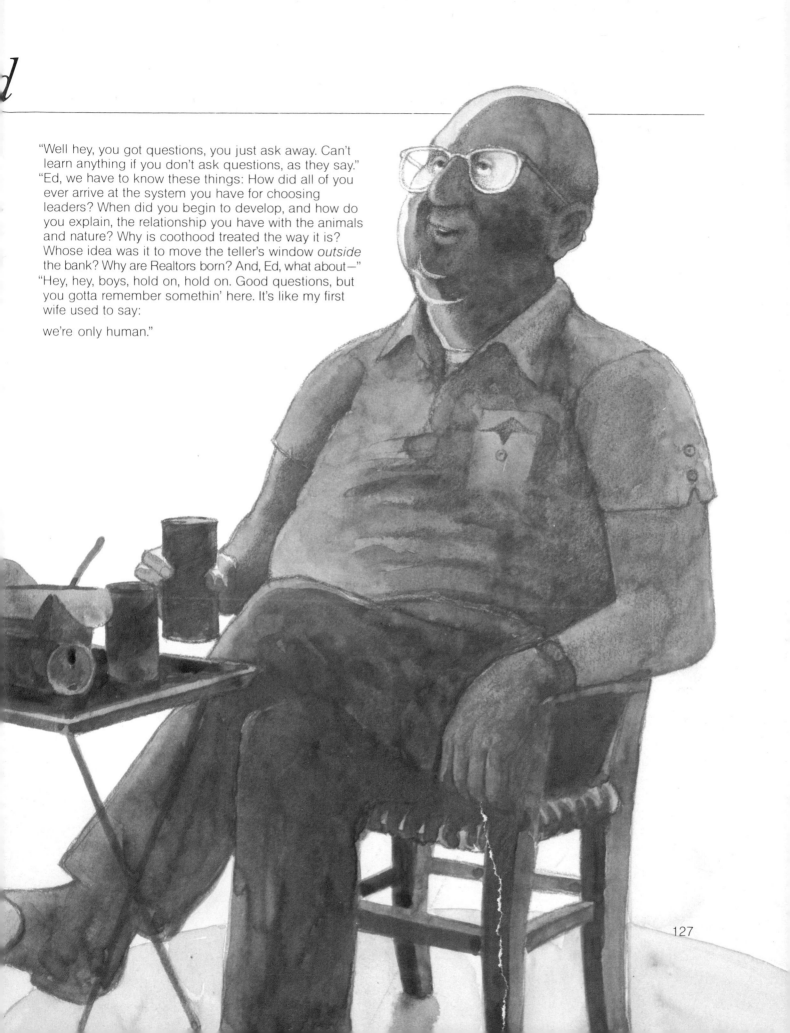

"Well hey, you got questions, you just ask away. Can't learn anything if you don't ask questions, as they say."

"Ed, we have to know these things: How did all of you ever arrive at the system you have for choosing leaders? When did you begin to develop, and how do you explain, the relationship you have with the animals and nature? Why is coothood treated the way it is? Whose idea was it to move the teller's window *outside* the bank? Why are Realtors born? And, Ed, what about—"

"Hey, hey, boys, hold on, hold on. Good questions, but you gotta remember somethin' here. It's like my first wife used to say:

we're only human."